CW00597109

A Year with Yours

Name	
Address	
Postcode	
Home phone	
Mobile phone	
Email	

In case of emergency, contact:

Name	
Telephone	

USEFUL CONTACTS

BANK	
BUILDING SOCIETY	
CHEMIST/PHARMACY	
CHIROPODIST	
COUNCIL	
CREDIT CARD EMERGENCY	
DENTIST	
DOCTOR	
ELECTRICIAN	
GARAGE	
HAIRDRESSER	
HOSPITAL	
LOCAL POLICE	
MILKMAN	
OPTICIAN	
PLUMBER	
SOLICITOR	
TAXI	
VET	

RENEWAL REMINDERS

	RENEWAL DATE	POLICY NUMBER	TELEPHONE
CAR INSURANCE			
CAR TAX			
MOT			
HOME INSURANCE			
TV LICENCE			
PET INSURANCE			
Yours SUBSCRIPTION			

The Year Ahead

A burst of golden sunshine

On the windswept coast of North Devon, a profusion of vibrant yellow blooms tumble down towards the sea. Covered in needle-like leaves and distinctive, coconut-scented flowers, common gorse is similar to its close relatives western gorse and dwarf gorse, but blooms in the first half of the year, from January to June, rather than in the latter. It can be seen in a variety of habitats, from wild heathland and coastal grasslands to towns and gardens, and provides shelter for many birds, including stonechats and Dartford warblers. Here, this prickly shrub dominates the view of Rockham Beach, near Ilfracombe, which has become known locally as Mortehoe Beach. It can only be visited at low tide, so tidal tables need to be checked before setting out, but a walk along the cliffs is equally rewarding. After the stark days of winter, an abundance of wild flowers emerge boldly and brightly, paving the way for the kaleidoscope of colours to come as spring takes hold, and the landscape awakens to the new season.

Beautiful Britain

Garden jobs

Simple steps to keep your plot looking good this season

RE-ENERGISE DAFFS

When your daff flowers start to fade, snip off their sorry-looking heads to tidy and to prevent them making seeds. This means they'll put all their energy and nutrients into replenishing the bulb for fabulous blooms next year. Let the leaves die back naturally before you remove them.

Restore vitamin D levels

Soaking up just 10-15 mins of sunlight daily, 25-40 mins for people with darker skin, during spring and summer helps to avoid vitamin D deficiency all year round, according to research. Head out into your garden around midday if you can and, while it may still be a bit chilly for shorts and t-shirts, roll up your sleeves and trousers for max effect and give your bones, teeth and muscles, as well as your mood, a boost.

FRESHEN UP POTS

If your patio plants have been in the same pots and soil for a number of years, chances are they could do with a refresh. Over time compost compacts and is stripped of nutrients, so you'll need to scrape off the top 5cm and replace it. First, cover with fresh peat-free compost and water. Then add a slow-release fertiliser (try Wilko All Purpose, £3.50/1kg, wilko.com) for an extra boost and add a top layer of grit, vermiculite, bark or small stones, to help drainage.

REHOME SELF SOWERS

Plants that sow their own seeds such as foxgloves save you time and money, but they don't always grow where you want them to. Now that the soil's warming up, it's a good time to move them. Dig up the roots, with some soil still around them, using a trowel and replant in a sunny or part-shaded spot. Water to help the roots settle into the soil and keep on watering until established.

Leave a few dandelions

If you're a neat-grass-lover, these self-seeders may be the bane of your lawn life. But the pollen and nectar-packed flowers provide an early all-you-can-eat buffet for masses of wildlife including bees, hoverflies and butterflies.

Supercharge roses

Just as their delicate buds start to form, now's the time to give these hungry plants a nutrient boost. Apply a general-purpose or rose fertiliser (try Miracle-Gro, £4.95/1L, diy.com) around the base of the shrub, followed by a generous layer of well-rotted garden compost or manure — leaving a 10cm gap around the stems because this could burn them and lead to rotting.

SOW SALAD LEAVES

You can't beat the fresh taste of lettuce and you'll save on supermarket prices too. They'll be happy in all sorts of pots — simply scatter seeds (try Lettuce Mix Salad Leaves, £1/1,400 seeds, wilko.com) thinly over multi-purpose compost, cover with a thin layer of compost, then place in a sunny spot. Keep them well watered and within 21 days they'll be ready for snipping, for you to enjoy in your salad.

Dot alliums around borders

Brighten things up with a few pot-grown alliums from your local garden centre. Give them a sunny spot in well-drained soil, digging in some coarse sand, grit or well-rotted garden compost first. For best effect, plant in odd groups of three or five. Water well.

Stunning
stately homes

After their winter repairs, spring sees many of the UK's marvellous mansions reopen their doors

WORLD HERITAGE CLASS

England's only non-royal, non-episcopal palace is Blenheim, in Oxfordshire, built on land gifted to John Churchill (the first Duke of Marlborough) by Queen Anne, and completed in 1722. Almost two centuries later it became the birthplace for his descendant Winston (who you just may have heard of!), and the estate now offers a special trail of the grounds to highlight places connected to the former Prime Minister, including the spot where he proposed to his future wife Clementine. No wonder it's classed as a UNESCO World Heritage Site. Now considered a masterpiece of Baroque architecture there's so much to see,

including gilded state rooms, secret passageways and a peek at how life was lived 'downstairs'. Children, meanwhile, will love the adventure playground. **Blenheimpalace.com**

Out & about

Forward thinking

We don't tend to think of historic homes as having mod-cons, but the eccentric Mount Stuart, on the tiny Isle of Bute in the Firth of Clyde, was

a pioneering pile from the start! It was the first home in Britain to boast an indoor heated swimming pool and was also quick on the uptake of electric lighting, central heating and an early telephone system. Built in the 19th Century (on the site of a damaged building from 1719) there's lots to admire inside, and a massive 300 acres of gardens to explore, which are home to globally significant plant collections. The venue also frequently hosts arts events and performances throughout the year. **Mountstuart.com**

A COLOURFUL HISTORY

Plas Newydd House and Gardens, Anglesey, has been standing in one shape or another since the 14th Century (though most of the house is from the 18th), and has since housed many marquesses, the famous artist Rex Whistler, and hundreds of cadets from HMS Conway. Be inspired by Whistler's 58ft mural and numerous artworks, explore the Grade I listed gardens, and hunt for red squirrels in its 129 acres of woodland. Mild conditions mean that rhododendrons and magnolias flourish, the borders are colourful from spring until autumn, and the woods host carpets of bluebells and daffodils. **Nationaltrust.org.uk**

A YORKSHIRE GEM

Gaze up at a 70ft high fresco of the four elements in the Dome of Castle Howard – you'll be left with a sense of awe, if perhaps a stiff neck! The baroque stately home, which took 100 years to complete, has been owned by the Howards for 300 years, and has seen not one but two versions of Brideshead Revisited filmed on site (in 1981 and 2008). The gardens are filled with monuments to hunt down, a mausoleum and an 18th Century pyramid. During the school holidays, take a boat trip across the North Lake to look for local wildlife; the area is home to plentiful birds, badgers and bats, to name a few. **Castlehoward.co.uk**

Darcy's digs

One of the country's most iconic stately homes is Chatsworth in Derbyshire. Dating back to the 16th Century, this classically beautiful spot was supposed to have inspired the fictional Pemberley, aka Mr Darcy's pad in Pride and Prejudice. In real life it's been owned for 16 generations of the lucky Devonshire family, and boasts 105 acres of gorgeous grounds to explore, including a Victorian rock garden. There's also a farmyard, where many animals can be fed and handled, and playground for little ones to enjoy. The venue plays host to a lively calendar of events, including arts and craft courses, exhibitions and activities for children. There are also numerous guided walks, many of which happen daily. **Chatsworth.org**

Create pretty hanging decorations

Perfect paper eggs

Bring the joys of springtime into your home with this 3D papercraft project

All materials available from Hobbycraft.co.uk

You will need...
Pack of A4 pastel coloured paper
White card
Brown jute twine
Black Fine Liner Pen
Pencil
Ruler
Scissors
Stix 2 in 1 Glue Pen
A4 Ruled Paper Sheet

1 Begin by drawing three different sized egg templates onto a piece of card (10.5, 9 and 7.5cm wide, as shown in the photo). Cut them out, then fold and crease them symmetrically in half.

2 Choose coloured paper from the pack. Make sure you have enough sheets for each egg: seven for the large egg, four for the medium egg, and three for the small egg.

3 Create a glueing guide on A4 ruled paper. Draw a solid black horizontal line towards the top of the page. Two lines below that, draw a dashed line. Repeat to match this image.

4 Take a sheet of coloured paper, fold up from the bottom and crease just enough paper to draw around the folded medium egg template with a pencil. Draw two and cut them out.

5 Repeat this process, working across the paper until you have cut eight eggs. Repeat for another three sheets until 28 egg pieces are cut. You should have two pieces spare.

6 Using the same process, the 35 large egg pieces can be cut from a diagonal fold. The 27 small egg pieces can be cut from folds along the longer edge of the paper.

7 Position one of your unfolded egg pieces onto the prepared glueing guide. Make sure the top is placed just above a dashed line, with a similar spacing of the solid line towards the bottom of the egg piece. Mark top and bottom with a pencil line. Use the glue pen to draw fine lines of glue from the centre fold line out to the edges. Place these lines of glue following only the dashed lines on the glueing guide. Fold the egg piece closed, and gently press flat. Repeat this process for all the other egg pieces.

8 Place one of the egg pieces back onto the glueing guide. Add lines of glue across the top surface, following the solid lines. Place another piece on top and press down. Repeat with the rest of the pieces.

9 Apply glue along the folded edge of the egg stack to hold the spine in place. Cut 26cm of twine and glue down the tails about three-quarters down the spine, leaving a loop at the top of the egg. Allow to dry.

10 Open out and secure your honeycomb eggs to form complete 3D shapes. Make several honeycomb eggs in all three sizes, using different coloured paper.

Flowers fit for a queen

Early morning light bursts through a woodland in north Lincolnshire, casting the frothy flowers of cow parsley in a luminous glow. A member of the carrot family, Anthriscus sylvestris is the most abundant and earliest flowering umbellifer, bearing delicate white blossoms in spring. It prefers dappled shade and is most commonly found adorning the fringes of woodland paths, roadside verges and hedgerows, forming dense clouds of effervescent blooms. This hollow-stemmed plant has many common names, including Queen Anne's lace. Some claim that Queen Anne travelled around the country in May and believed the roadsides had been specifically decorated for her. Another story suggests that she suffered from asthma and would take walks in the countryside for some fresh air, passing the flowers, which reminded her of the delicate lace pillows her ladies-in-waiting carried, thus creating this name for them.

Garden jobs

Simple steps to keep your plot looking good this season

SPACE FOR SALAD

Any gaps left by crops such as early spuds can quickly and easily be plugged by lush gem lettuce leaves for sweet flavoursome pickings for summer salads. Our favourite is the variety 'Moon Red' with deep red outer leaves and a green heart.

PRETTIFY YOUR POND

A waterlily in full flower will bring colour to your pond. You can buy them in aquatic planting baskets filled with aquatic compost. Top with gravel or pebbles and lower into the pond so the base of the stems are 20cm under water and the leaves are floating on the surface.

Summer gardening

Holiday proof pots

Make sure your pot plants don't miss you while you're away by moving them to a shady place so they won't dry out as quickly in hot spells. Try to avoid 'rain shadows' where the plants end up sheltered from the rain. And remember to water them well before you go.

BRING IN THE BIRDS

Seeing or hearing birds can make us feel chirpier, according to research from King's College London. So if you haven't already, now's a great time to invite more birdsong into your garden. Put out extra food on a bird table or feeder and plant flowers and long grasses to attract insects, including butterflies and moths, which produce caterpillars and provide plenty of prey for birds and their chicks to feed on. Even a small patch will be beneficial.

TACKLE APHIDS

These pests will love tasty summer leaves so keep a look out for them and rub them off by hand. Or you could encourage aphid-eating hoverflies into your garden by adding the plants they love such as cosmos, yarrow, dill and marigolds.

Water less this summer

Spend more time on your sunlounger and less time can-in-hand by thoroughly soaking plants when the compost or soil is dry and adding a 5cm layer of an organic mulch such as bark chippings. You could also add mulch just after a rainy spell.

Boost fuchsias

Cut the tips of the longest stems back to the next pair of leaves using snips, or pinch them off by hand for lots more sideshoots and flowers.

FEED BASKETS

Your hanging baskets are up, but to keep them full of colour and lasting well into autumn, they'll need regular feeding and watering. Choose a plant food that contains more potassium than phosphorous and nitrogen for a bloom boost (try Flower Power Premium Plant Food, richardjacksonsgarden.co.uk). Feed once a week now until early autumn, making sure the compost never fully dries out.

Take the plunge

Warmer weather means it's time to make a splash in an outdoor swimming pool

BUDE SEA POOL

For a taste of sea-swimming without the challenges of battling strong currents, you can't do better than the semi-natural tidal pool at Bude, Cornwall. Even better – it's free to use, although donations are encouraged by the charity that runs it (Friends of Bude Sea Pool). As you'd imagine, being filled by water from the Atlantic Ocean means the temperature can vary, reaching highs of around 18°C in the summer. But perhaps more surprisingly, being tidal also means the depths in the pool change, depending on how much sand the tide brings in! It's roughly 91m long, so there's plenty of room to practise your breaststroke. **Budeseapool.org**

Stonehaven Open Air Pool

The UK's only art deco Olympic-sized sea water lido is in Aberdeenshire, and was opened in 1934 as a bathing facility for locally based troops during the Second World War. It's a more luxurious affair now thanks to being heated, and runs sessions for children, with a paddling pool for younger ones. Events include quiet swims, Zumba classes, inflatables sessions and entertainment at weekends, plus there is a café and free parking. There's full wheelchair access, a hoist and assistance for those with special needs, while carers can swim for free. **stonehavenopenairpool.co.uk**

Saltdean Lido

Nothing warms the cockles quite like a story about a community coming together to save a local spot. Saltdean Lido, outside Brighton, is one such. Having been earmarked to become flats in 2010, locals banded together to protect and restore the pool, which dates back to 1937. It has a unique crescent shape, is 40m long and heated, and has a grassy area for you to relax or sunbathe. Now that it's being so well supported, it is in high demand and hosts lots of quirky events – from yoga to an annual doggy dip. Little ones will enjoy the children's splash pool, which has fountains and is always supervised by a lifeguard. Hardy swimming addicts will be pleased to know the lido also opens for most weekends over the winter too! **saltdeanlido.co.uk**

LIDO PONTY

Known as the 'national lido of Wales', and a former favourite spot for a young would-be pop star called Tom Jones, Lido Ponty, Pontypridd, has been beloved by al fresco dippers since it was built in 1927. It helps that, since then, it's had a fantastic £6.3m spent to help restore it to its former glory, maintaining and upgrading its charming original features such as wooden changing cabins and Twenties turnstiles. It now also boasts Lido Play, an adventure play area for kids, and a visitor centre where you can discover more about its fascinating history. The true heroes are, of course, its three heated swimming pools, but special mention must go to its Waffle House café where you can refuel post-dip. **rctcbc.gov.uk/EN/Resident/SportsandLeisure/Lido**

Peterborough Lido

This art deco-styled lido first welcomed local swimmers in 1936 and has been popular ever since – even more so since adding heating to its 50m pool! It's Grade II listed, and is one of the finest remaining examples of the 'hacienda-style' design in the UK. There's a separate children's teaching pool, a paddling pool, a café, sun terrace and grassy area. It hosts a variety of events over the summer, including film nights, fitness classes (Zumba and yoga), a dog swim and a summer solstice event when it opens before sunrise and closes after sunset. In recent years the lido has opened earlier in the year and remained open into the autumn or winter too. **vivacity.org/sports-venues/peterborough-lido**

Over the rainbow

Learn how to make this beautiful cushion with our beginner's guide to punch needling

All materials available from Hobbycraft.co.uk

You will need...
A punch needle set
Sewing needle and white thread
A tapestry frame with clips

Scissors
Fabric marker pen
2 x pieces of white cotton fabric measuring at least 45 x 45cm
Rowan felted tweed yarn in your choice of rainbow colours
Polyester stuffing

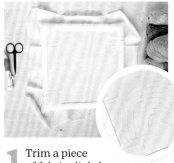

1 Trim a piece of fabric slightly larger than your tapestry frame, around 45 x 45cm. Stretch your fabric over the frame and secure with the clips. Using a marker pen, trace your shape straight onto the fabric.

2 Choose the colour you want to start with – we chose pink. Thread your punch needle following the instructions in the leaflet provided in the punch needle set. Complete one row following the design on the fabric.

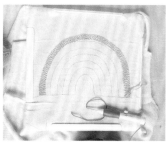

3 Repeat this until you have 10 lines of pink stitching, making sure the lines are close together and the stitches are neat and consistent. Once you have finished with the pink, trim the wool leaving about 10cm.

4 Repeat step 3 until you have filled in the whole of your rainbow using different colours. Each colour has 10 rows of stitching. Next, using your wool needle, thread all the ends through to the other side.

5 Turn your frame over and you will see all the loops you have created. You might need to trim a few loops that are a little longer than others. Also you will need to trim the strands you have just sewn through.

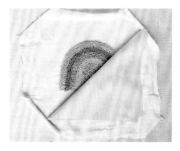

6 Once you've finished and are happy with your loops, cut a piece of fabric to create the back of your cushion. The backing fabric needs to measure about 30 x 30cm. Pin the two right sides together.

7 Sew around the edges leaving a 1cm seam allowance. Remember to leave a 10cm hole so you can turn your cushion the right side out and have an opening so you can stuff it.

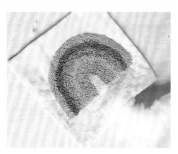

8 Stuff your cushion to your desired firmness. Make sure you get stuffing in each of the corners. Once you are happy with the stuffing, sew up the 10cm hole using a needle and matching thread.

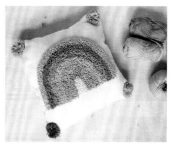

9 To finish off, add a little decoration by making and sewing different coloured pom poms to each corner of the cushion using the matching colours from the rainbow.

Autumn's golden hour

As the days shorten, skies can appear bolder and brighter. During sunrise and sunset, they glimmer with the most spectacular hues, from blooming pinks to fiery reds, and every shade of orange, yellow and purple. Beautiful at any time, these golden hours are particularly radiant during autumn and winter. Meteorologists suggest this is due to the angle of the sun, cloud factors and humidity. The sun rises and sets at a shallower angle, and light passes through much more of the atmosphere before reaching the eyes. Short-wave blue rays cannot travel very far and are usually scattered, while red and orange can travel further, becoming more pronounced. Therefore, the sky appears pinker and redder than usual. The air is also less humid, so the colours seem more vivid, and the clouds are higher, reflecting them for longer. Here, a solitary boathouse, on the shores of Ullswater in Cumbria, glows in the early morning light; a rose-tinted sunrise reflected in the still waters like a liquid imprint.

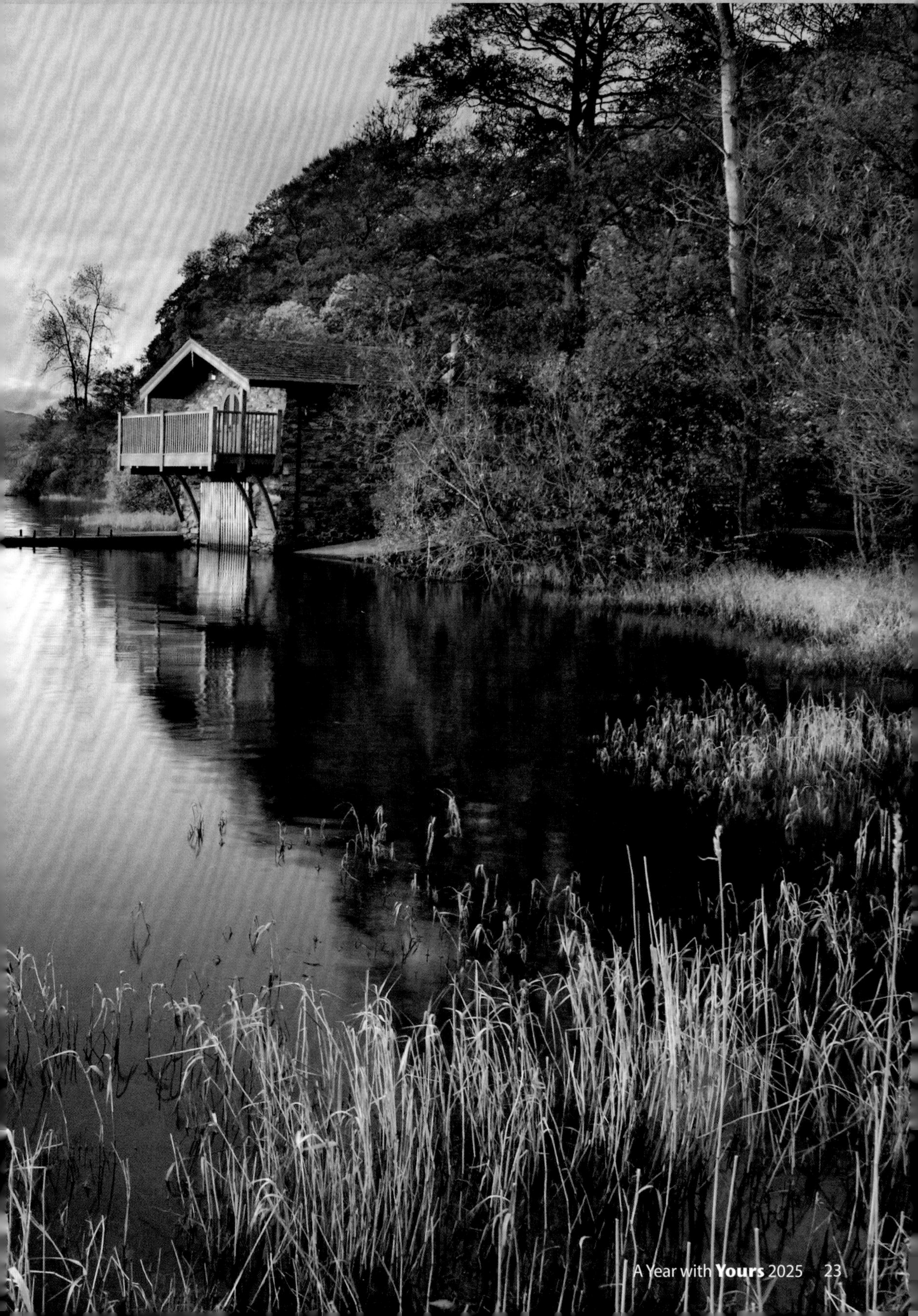

Garden jobs

Simple steps to keep your plot looking good this season

PICK UP SOME WINTER PANSIES

Trays of these cheery winter bloomers will be filling up garden centre shelves right now, so why not grab a couple for pots or beds? Plant straight away while the ground is still warm so they can settle in before the cold weather arrives. Deadhead to keep them flowering until spring.

ACE ALSTROEMERIAS

Keep them blooming for longer, into November, by pulling out the stems from the base of the plant when flowers fade. Add a layer of compost around the base of the plant to protect roots from frosts.

Autumn gardening

Skip over the hips

Don't be too eager to snip off seed heads as flowers fade. Not only can their intricate shapes add a new dimension to your garden, but they can also provide food and shelter for wildlife. Thrushes, blackbirds and redwings will flock to your rose hips.

PACK IN THE 'MUMS'

You can't beat them for a dazzling patio display this time of year, so plant up a button-flowered ball chrysanthemum. They prefer well-drained loamy compost such as John Innes No.2 and need planting at the same depth in their new pot as they were in the previous one. Give them a sunny spot and water well until settled in.

BLAST AWAY DEBRIS

If you find pressure washing as satisfying as we do, you won't need an excuse to give your patio and paths a going over. Get rid of moss, algae or dirt that could make them slippy in autumn by brushing with a stiff broom, trim back plants to allow in more light to discourage algae growth, then blast!

Bring in the bulbs

Get spring-flowering bulbs – think daffs, crocuses and hyacinths – in the ground so they can nestle in and develop roots before winter. Plant in sun or part-shade in well-drained soil in the ground or compost in pots.

TOUGHEN YOUR LAWN

Give your grass a feed now to strengthen it against winter weather and any drought next summer. Use a high-potash autumn feed such as Miracle-Gro Evergreen Autumn Lawn Care Feed, £24, amazon.co.uk.

Hang herbs to dry

Stock up on supplies for winter dishes by picking herbs before summer comes to an end. Tie in bunches, hang up to dry and pop in airtight jars after 2-3 days. Keep in a cool dry place.

SAVE SWEET-PEA SEEDS

If your sweet peas have done you proud this summer, why not collect the seeds for a free display next year? Wait until the seed pods are brown and brittle and, on a dry day, pick and put on a tray in a dry place. Cover with paper because the pods will twist when dry and fling the seeds out. Store in paper envelopes to sow in spring – or sow later.

GRIZEDALE FOREST

If you go down to the woods today, you're sure of a big surprise... Not picnicking bears, but a wealth of jewel shades as Grizedale Forest, in Cumbria, turns red, orange and gold all over its 4,000 acres. Nestled in the Lake District National Park, it has a range of enticing walks including peaceful valleys, ancient beech trees and remarkable views across mountains and lakes. Keep your eyes peeled for more than 50 sculptures by some of the art world's biggest names (including Andy Goldsworthy) dotted between the trees. There are also cycling and horse-riding trails if you'd like to see the world from a different angle. Animal lovers should keep their eyes peeled for the UK's only remaining herd of indigenous red deer, while bird enthusiasts can spot barn owls, red kites and buzzards.
Forestryengland.uk/grizedale

Autumn colour

Nature loves to put on a show at this time of year – here's where to enjoy it

MONMOUTHSHIRE AND BRECON CANAL

Affectionately known as the Mon and Brec Canal, this lovely Powys waterway has 36 miles to explore on foot, bike or, of course, on a narrowboat. Much of it is lined by gorgeous beech trees that are golden at this time of year, and double the value as they are reflected back at you. There is a wealth of routes to walk, as well as lots of industrial history to discover, such as old lime kilns. Wildlife-wise, be on the lookout for red kites, buzzards, herons, otters and water voles. You can take a public cruise by narrowboat from Brecon Basin to Brynich Lock for brilliant views of the Central Beacons and the River Usk. **Canalrivertrust.org.uk**

THE HERMITAGE, NEAR DUNKELD

This Perthshire spot is glorious in autumn, thanks to its colourful deciduous firs, birches, hazels and oaks. It also has evergreens, including one of the tallest Douglas firs in the country, and natural drama – look out for active salmon leaping in the waterfalls. Go for a woodland ramble to the pretty folly of Ossian's Hall and look down at the Black Linn waterfall. Or take a moment of tranquillity on the Douglas fir bench — designed to allow walkers to lie back and look up at the majestic tall trees above, where the Douglas firs make a 'cathedral' roof overhead. You might even be lucky enough to spot a red squirrel or two while you are there. **Nts.org.uk**

WESTONBIRT ARBORETUM

Known as the 'national arboretum', it's no wonder that Westonbirt, in Gloucestershire, is packed with beautiful trees – in fact, there are more than 2,500 varieties planted here. It's one of the world's most important collections, dating back 200 years, with 15,000 specimens. So, naturally, autumn is a colourful affair! Explore a tree-top walkway for a bird's-eye view of the season, follow a soothing wellbeing trail, or choose one of the guided or self-led walks. **Forestryengland.uk/westonbirt -the-national-arboretum**

Wicken Fen

When you think of autumn colour, it's probably woodlands that spring to mind. But there can be as much drama to be found in alternative landscapes — the Fens being a prime example. Wicken Fen Nature Reserve in Cambridgeshire is at its finest in September, when the sedge turns russet and golden. Bird lovers will be in their element: look out for flashes of blue as kingfishers dart in and out of the water, while huge numbers of wigeon arrive at this time of year. From October, wintering fieldfare and redwing flock to the reserve to feast on the hedgerow berries. Hen harriers arrive for the season too, and short-eared owls can be spotted doing some daytime hunting. The reserve is also home to beautiful Konik ponies, which help manage the site as they graze, and their water-filled hoofprints and manure help to attract new species of flora and fauna. **Nationaltrust.org.uk**

All strung up

Give your home an autumnal makeover with this pretty felt leaf garland

All materials are available from Hobbycraft.co.uk

You will need...

1 x A4 felt sheet in the following colours: burgundy, cream, yellow, light brown and dark brown
Embroidery needle
DMC embroidery threads in your choice of contrasting colours
Scissors
Pen/pencil
Cardboard

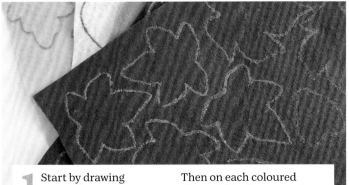

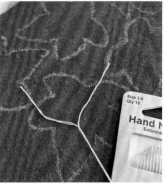

1 Start by drawing yourself several different leaf templates in various sizes on a piece of card (we used eight designs).

Then on each coloured sheet of felt, draw round the leaf templates, using a variety of styles for each colour of felt.

2 Take your first embroidery thread colour and split the strands so you have two sets of three strands each. Thread a needle.

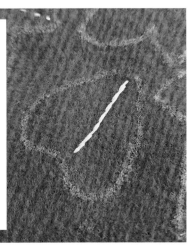

3 Now it's time to start the embroidery of your leaves. Embroider directly onto the felt. If you feel the need to place a hoop around it you can, but be careful not to stretch the felt. Use the photo (left) as a guide for the embroidery. We used the following stitches (you can find tutorials online): running stitch, stem stitch, back stitch, chain stitch and French knots.

4 Once you've added the embroidery details to each leaf, carefully cut out each one.

5 Place your leaves in a line to determine the order you want them to hang in. Once happy you can take a 2.5m piece of six-stranded embroidery thread and use a needle to thread through all the leaves, then tie a knot at each end to secure them.

6 And there you have it, you have created a simple but beautiful piece of autumn home décor!

Dazzling rings

At Christmastime, the melodious notes of *The Twelve Days of Christmas* echo in churches and through streets decked in festive green and cranberry red. The carol features many birds, including seven swans a-swimming, six geese a-laying, three French hens, two turtle doves and a partridge in a pear tree. Some theories suggest the lyric 'five gold rings' may also allude to another bird: the pheasant. While this is unlikely, since the first published version of the song, in 1780, shows an illustration of five rings, fitting for the Georgian period, pheasants have long been associated with Christmas. The males bear a rich chestnut and golden-brown plumage, with black markings, and an iridescent green head, red face wattling, and a distinctive, bold white ring. Females are typically less colourful, with a mottled plumage in buff and black. Both have a long, pointed tail, with striped feathers. Some suggest the pheasant symbolises prosperity and fertility.

Garden jobs

Simple steps to keep your plot looking good this season

MAKE YOUR OWN COMPOST

Sweep up dead tree leaves and turn them into leaf mould, a black crumbly garden treat that makes a good soil improver or mulch. Jute leaf bags (£7.95/2, sarahraven.com) make light and quick work of the decomposing process. Simply sweep the leaves into the bags, wet them well and store in a corner of the garden until next winter.

CHECK YOUR HOUSEPLANTS

While they may not be in full growing mode in winter, houseplants still need enough light. Move them closer to a source of light, avoid placing plants that are used to shade in direct sun, and be aware that a windowsill may be too cold. Dust the leaves with a soft cloth, too, to ensure they can fully absorb the sunlight.

Leave hydrangea heads

It can be tempting to snip off browning flowerheads to neaten them up but it's best to keep them in place until spring to protect stems from frost. Mopheads in particular produce flowers from the stem tips grown the previous summer, so frost damage can reduce flower power. Wait until late March/April, when the worst of the icy weather has passed. Plus they look super-pretty all frosty!

HELP HYACINTHS LAST FOR LONGER

Keep these Christmas favourites in a cool room – if they're too warm, the flowers won't last long and the stems will flop. A windowsill is fine because chilly nights won't harm them, and keep the compost moist. After flowering, put the pot outside in a sheltered spot or plant the bulbs in your garden while still growing, in a sunny spot. They'll bloom next year as long as you let them die down naturally.

Stop ponds freezing over

To prevent the surface of your pond from freezing solid, to let oxygen in and toxic gases out, place a tennis ball in the water.

BUY BARGAIN BULBS

Prime time for spring bulb planting has passed, but it's not too late to plant some last-minute bargain buys in pots. You should find on-sale bulbs in garden centres and supermarkets, but give them a gentle squeeze and discard any soft ones. Add a handful of grit to the compost to ensure good drainage in this torrential weather!

Display your seedheads

Statuesque allium stems, particularly Allium cristophii, look wonderful in winter. Hand-pick a bunch from your plot for a dried flower display to brighten a room or use as a festive table centrepiece.

EMBRACE THE SNOW

We all love a bit of snow to ramp up that festive feeling, but did you know the white stuff can also be good for your wellbeing?

Psychotherapist Noel Bell says it's a good sound absorber, making the world more peaceful; the sound of falling snow can mimic a white-noise machine, shown to help with relaxation and reducing stress levels; and it can encourage us to tap in to our inner child, playing outdoors, enjoying the moment and becoming more mindful. So if you get any snow, why not take time out to build a snowman, throw a few snowballs or just sit and listen to it falling?

Quirky
museums

Staying indoors is anything but boring at the country's most unique collections

A LEADING LIGHT

If you have romantic notions about coastal living (or just an enthusiasm for stair climbing!) the Museum of Scottish Lighthouses, Fraserburgh, is worth a visit. Not least as it's situated within a 16th Century castle (Kinnaird Head Castle), which features a full-sized lighthouse built inside it. This strange design came about in 1787 when the castle was sold to the Northern Lighthouse Board and converted into the country's first mainland lighthouse. The castle itself features several other original features to explore, including historic kitchens. You'll learn about the lives of the lighthouse keepers, what it was like to run one, and all about the sophisticated technology that was developed to save lives. It's open Wednesday to Sunday with tours on the hour. Tickets cost £11 for adults, £5 for children. **lighthousemuseum.org.uk**

Delight in Doctor Who

Calling all science fiction fanatics – get yourselves to the Museum of Classic Sci-Fi, in Allendale, Northumberland, and you're in for a real treat. Here you can discover the history of classic Doctor Who and general sci-fi from H.G. Wells onwards, through original props, costumes and artwork. Comic book enthusiasts will get a kick out of animated cells and other items connected to Marvel cartoons and films, while there are also several unique items from the Star Wars saga, including an Ewok mask from Return of the Jedi. This has all come about through one man's passion (curator Neil Cole) who not only collects, but restores and preserves these precious items. There are often special exhibitions too. It's open Friday to Monday year-round, and costs £7 for adults, with under-fives going free. **museumofclassicsci-fi.com**

FRENCH FANCY

While Reading Museum itself is traditional in its focus (Roman history, medieval carvings, artworks, etc) it does boast one quirky item that's particularly worth a visit – a full-sized replica of the Bayeux Tapestry, depicting the events of 1066. It was made in the 1880s, after skilled embroiderer Elizabeth Wardle visited the original and decided we needed our own version. She, and 35 women from the Leek Embroidery Society, picked up their needles and delivered just that... or, almost, anyway. Either the modest women themselves, or perhaps those who had given them photos to copy, decided there was too much nudity in the original, so the Reading Museum version features tiny embroidered pants! The museum is free, plus it saves you the cost of travelling to France to see the original.
readingmuseum.org.uk

Bang to rights

If you're a fan of crime dramas, you'll no doubt be fascinated by the real-life tales of the Greater Manchester Police Museum. Small but mighty, the building was once a functioning police station, and now houses archives about the city's police, with plenty of interesting exhibits. Discover more about the history of women in policing, why the uniform looks the way it does, and admire a vintage police box. The volunteers, all former members of the Force, are great at bringing history to life, and will even put you in the court dock for misbehaving (or for a photo opportunity!) It's open for free every Tuesday from 10.30am – 3.30pm, while private tours can be arranged on other days.
gmpmuseum.co.uk

MYTHS AND MAGIC

For a decidedly spooky experience, pop into the Morbitorium, which proudly declares itself, 'Wales' weirdest day out.' It may physically be 30 minutes from Cardiff (in Pontywaun), but in a sense it's a world away, as it's packed to the rafters with the strange and mysterious. From haunted Ouija boards to mummified cats, antique medical contraptions to human skulls, it's not for the faint-hearted. But if you're keen on horror, the macabre, or simply looking for something off the beaten track, it's a day you're sure to remember. Open daily except Wed and Sun. Adults, £2.50, under-16s free.
morbitorium.co.uk

Away in a manger

Make this adorable nativity scene using craft or loo rolls

All materials available from Hobbycraft.co.uk

You will need...
A small cardboard box (like a cereal box)
A selection of cardboard tubes
Glue stick
Paints and paintbrushes

Pencil
Ruler
Scissors
Black and white paint marker/ felt tip pens
Felt in assorted colours

Black and metallic coloured paper
Pipe cleaners in a range of colours
Handful of small white pom poms

Seasonal crafts

1 First make the stable. Using a pencil and ruler, draw, measure and cut a front opening in the box with two diagonal struts on each of the top corners. Fold the front open flat.

2 Next, paint the stable beige, and leave to dry before adding a second coat.

3 Cut a square of black paper for the window and draw on some lines in white pen. Add a gold star with glue and stick the window to the inside of the stable.

4 To make the characters, cut the tubes to size: 5cm for the sheep and donkey, 8cm for Mary, 9cm for the angel and shepherd, and 10cm for Joseph and the Kings. Paint the tubes and leave to dry.

5 Cut and stick 5cm wide pieces of felt around each of the bottom sections of Mary, Joseph, the shepherd, angel and Three Kings.

6 Cut out rectangular felt head scarves for Mary, Joseph and the shepherd, and glue to the tops of the tubes.

7 Make a crook for the shepherd with a beige pipe cleaner and add a brown pipe cleaner 'beard' to Joseph. Then make 'baby Jesus' with cream felt and pink paper and stick to Mary's body. Draw eyes, noses and mouths with the black pen.

8 For the Kings' crowns, cut out 2cm wide strips of gold card and draw 1cm wide triangles along one side of each. Cut out the triangles and wrap the strips around the tops of each tube – trim and glue in place. Stick pipe cleaner beards to the faces, and then draw eyes, noses and mouths with a black pen.

9 For the angel, first stick a piece of cream felt 'hair' to her head – cut it shorter at the front and snip along the edge to create a fringe. Then cut a 5cm wide piece of white felt for her wings and cut a scalloped edge on each end. Wrap it around the body and glue in place. Make a silver tinsel pipe cleaner 'halo' and glue to the back of her head. Then add eyes, nose and mouth with the black pen.

10 Finally, to make the sheep and donkey, cut and glue some felt ears to the top of the brown and white tubes. Add black pipe cleaner 'hair' to the donkey, and white pom pom 'coat' to the sheep. As before, draw the eyes, nose and mouth with the black pen.

Notable dates 2025

New Year's Day (Bank Holiday)	Wednesday January 1
Bank Holiday (Scotland)	Thursday January 2
Epiphany	Monday January 6
Burns Night	Saturday January 25
Chinese New Year (Snake)	Wednesday January 29
Valentine's Day	Friday February 14
First Day of Ramadan (Islam)	Friday February 28
St David's Day	Saturday March 1
Shrove Tuesday (Pancake Day)	Tuesday March 4
Ash Wednesday	Wednesday March 5
St Patrick's Day (Bank Holiday N. Ireland)	Monday March 17
British Summer Time begins (clocks go forward)	Sunday March 30
Mothering Sunday	Sunday March 30
First Day of Passover (Jewish Holiday)	Saturday April 12
Palm Sunday	Sunday April 13
Maundy Thursday	Thursday April 17
Good Friday (Bank Holiday)	Friday April 18
Easter Sunday	Sunday April 20
Easter Monday (Bank Holiday except Scotland)	Monday April 21
St George's Day	Wednesday April 23
May Day (Early May Bank Holiday)	Monday May 5
Spring Bank Holiday	Monday May 26
Ascension Day	Thursday May 29
Father's Day	Sunday June 15
Summer Solstice (Longest day)	Saturday June 21
Islamic New Year	Thursday June 26
Armed Forces Day	Saturday June 28
American Independence Day	Friday July 4
Battle of the Boyne	Saturday July 12
Battle of the Boyne (Bank Holiday N. Ireland)	Monday July 14
St Swithin's Day	Tuesday July 15
Summer Bank Holiday (Scotland)	Monday August 4
Summer Bank Holiday (Except Scotland)	Monday August 25
Jewish New Year (Rosh Hashanah)	Monday September 22
Diwali (Hindu Festival)	Monday October 20
Trafalgar Day	Tuesday October 21
British Summer Time ends (clocks go back)	Sunday October 26
Halloween	Friday October 31
All Saints' Day	Saturday November 1
Guy Fawkes Night	Wednesday November 5
Remembrance Sunday	Sunday November 9
St Andrew's Day	Sunday November 30
First Sunday in Advent	Sunday November 30
St Andrew's Day (Bank Holiday Scotland)	Monday December 1
Winter Solstice (Shortest day)	Sunday December 21
Christmas Day (Bank Holiday)	Thursday December 25
Boxing Day (Bank Holiday)	Friday December 26
New Year's Eve/Hogmanay	Wednesday December 31

The Year Ahead

29	SUNDAY	

30	MONDAY	

31	TUESDAY	

1	WEDNESDAY	*New Year's Day (Bank Holiday)*

2	THURSDAY	*Bank Holiday (Scotland)*

3	FRIDAY	

4	SATURDAY	

CLEVER CLEANING TIPS

Say goodbye to sticky labels

Want to re-use glass bottles and jars but can't get the label glue residue off them? Simply dab a bit of white vinegar on a cloth and gently wipe the surface, then mix a couple of teaspoons of bicarbonate of soda with a few drops of water to create a paste. Use this to gently agitate the glue, et voilà! Your bottles and jars will be clean, clear and ready to use.

WISE WORDS

'To plant a garden is to believe in tomorrow.'
Audrey Hepburn

REMEMBER THIS

Woollen wonders

Winter was full of challenges, not least the prospect of being forced to try out Mum and Granny's latest homemade knits for the first time. We had watched in horror as we saw these itchy, scratchy, often oversized creations gradually developing as our nearest and dearest worked away on them during the year. Thankfully, they were at least always warm!

Recipe of the week

LEEK, HAM & BRUSSELS SPROUT GRATIN

SERVES: **4** PREP TIME: **5 mins** COOK TIME: **45 mins**

Oil, for frying
3 leeks, thickly sliced (white and green parts)
250g (9oz) Brussels sprouts – tough ends removed and finely sliced
60g (2oz) butter
50g (2oz) plain flour
500ml (18 fl oz) milk
2 tsp Dijon mustard
100g (4oz) grated Cheddar cheese (plus extra for the topping)
200g (7oz) baked ham, cut into small pieces
Salt and pepper

1. Heat the oven to 200°C/180°C Fan/Gas Mark 6. Meanwhile, heat a drizzle of oil in a large non-stick pan with a lid. Add the leeks and shredded sprouts and fry on a medium heat for 5 mins, stirring regularly and placing the lid on the pan in between.
2. Place the leeks and sprouts in an ovenproof dish. Melt the butter in the frying pan, then stir in the flour on medium heat until it starts to bubble.
3. Slowly add the milk a little at a time, bringing to the boil before adding more and stirring continuously.
4. Stir in the mustard, grated cheese and ham. Season with salt and pepper.
5. Pour the cheese sauce over the veg and stir well.
6. Top with the extra grated cheese and bake in the oven for 30 mins until golden brown.

BRITISH LEEKS

5	SUNDAY	

6	MONDAY	*Epiphany*

7	TUESDAY	

8	WEDNESDAY	

9	THURSDAY	

10	FRIDAY	

11	SATURDAY	

CLEVER CLEANING TIPS

Remove fingerprints from stainless steel in a flash

Dip a clean cloth in baby oil and rub it all over your stainless steel surface to see any smudges or fingerprints vanish.

WISE WORDS
'Keep your face toward the sunshine and shadows will fall behind you.'
Walt Whitman

REMEMBER THIS

Snowball fights
There were always people down at the park, especially on snow days. Usually, we knew them: there were a lot of children growing up down our way. But sometimes it would be a new face, someone unfamiliar. That didn't matter a jot. As long as they could build a slide and were up for a snowball fight, they were OK as far as we were concerned.

Recipe of the week

VEGAN BEAN AND CALIFORNIA WALNUT BUDDHA BOWLS

SERVES: **2** PREP TIME: **15 mins** COOK TIME: **8 mins**

Juice 1 lemon
1½ tbsp extra virgin olive oil, plus 2 tsp
3 tsp maple syrup
1 tsp Dijon mustard
150g (5oz) Brussels sprouts, trimmed and thinly sliced
1 carrot, cut into ribbons
150g (5oz) frozen green beans
75g (3oz) California walnuts
1 tsp pul biber seasoning, plus extra for serving
½ thick slice wholemeal bread, cubed
400g (14oz) can cannellini beans, drained and rinsed

1. Make the dressing by whisking the lemon juice, 1 tbsp oil, 2 tsp maple syrup and mustard together. Season, then mix 1½ tbsp of the dressing into the sprouts and carrot ribbons and massage gently with your hands for a minute to soften. Set aside.
2. Blanch the green beans in simmering water for 3 mins, drain and refresh under cold water.
3. Heat ½ tbsp oil in a small frying pan and fry the walnuts with the remaining maple syrup and pul biber for 1-2 mins to caramelise, then set aside.
4. Heat the remaining 2 tsp oil in the same pan and fry the bread cubes for 2-3 mins until golden and crisp.
5. Place the sprout and carrot ribbons, cannellini beans, green beans and walnuts in piles around 2 shallow bowls, drizzle over the dressing and top with the croutons to serve.

CALIFORNIA WALNUT

12	SUNDAY

13	MONDAY

14	TUESDAY

15	WEDNESDAY

16	THURSDAY

17	FRIDAY

18	SATURDAY

CLEVER CLEANING TIPS

Get a streak-free TV

Cleaning a TV screen can be tricky, and you want to avoid liquid if at all possible. Try using a dryer sheet. These will leave the screen streak-free and they're anti-static which will cut down on polishing time later.

WISE WORDS

'In the depth of winter I finally learned that there was in me an invincible summer.'
Albert Camus

REMEMBER THIS

The bigger the better!

The idea was to build the biggest snowball ever. We imagined it would gather up everything in its path as it rolled down the hill – more snow, people, trees – like they do in the comics. Somehow it didn't quite work out and we gave up, exhausted. The giant snowball was still there, a week after the big thaw.

Recipe of the week

CAULIFLOWER PAKORAS WITH MANGO RAITA

SERVES: **6** PREP TIME: **10 mins** COOK TIME: **10 mins**

6 heaped tbsp plain Greek yoghurt
A large handful of coriander, chopped (optional)
2 heaped tbsp Tracklements Indian Mango Chutney
Sea salt and freshly ground black pepper
150g (5oz) gram flour (chickpea flour)
½ tsp baking powder
2 tsp ground cumin
2 tsp ground coriander
½ tsp ground turmeric
Generous pinch cayenne pepper
½ tsp sea salt
1 medium-large cauliflower (about 800g), trimmed and cut into bite-sized pieces
Sunflower oil, for frying

1. Start by making the raita. Mix the yoghurt, handful of coriander and chutney together, seasoning with salt and pepper to taste. Chill.
2. For the batter, put the gram flour, baking powder, ground spices, cayenne pepper and salt into a large bowl.
3. Mix gently to get rid of any lumps. Slowly whisk in 175ml (6 fl oz) cold water to make a smooth batter. Add more water if needed; different brands of flour will vary in how much they absorb – err on the side of 'thicker'.
4. Add the cauliflower florets to the batter making sure they are thoroughly coated.
5. Heat about a 1cm depth of oil in a heavy-based pan over a medium-high heat. When the oil is hot enough to turn a cube of white bread light golden brown in 30-40 secs, start cooking the pakoras, a few at a time. Place spoonfuls of battered cauliflower – a few florets per spoonful – into the oil. Cook for about 2 mins, until crisp and golden brown on the base, then turn over with a slotted spoon and cook for another 1-2 mins.
6. Drain the pakoras on kitchen paper, then serve piping hot with the raita for dipping.

TRACKLEMENTS

19	SUNDAY

20	MONDAY

21	TUESDAY

22	WEDNESDAY

23	THURSDAY

24	FRIDAY

25	SATURDAY	*Burns Night*

CLEVER CLEANING TIPS

Get the shine back in your cutlery

Mix bicarbonate of soda with a little water to form a paste. Spread this all over your forks, knives and spoons to achieve sparkling silverware.

WISE WORDS

'Success is not final, failure is not fatal: it is the courage to continue that counts.'
Winston Churchill

REMEMBER THIS?

Sick days

Nobody likes being sick, but there was certainly an upside to the situation. A day off school spent in the company of Dan Dare, Robot Archie or Roy of the Rovers, in a state of total relaxation while receiving an endless supply of drinks or the occasional bowl of chicken soup? Things could certainly have been worse!

Recipe of the week

TOFFEE APPLE CRUMBLE

SERVES: **6** PREP TIME: **15 mins** COOK TIME: **30 mins**

150g (5oz) toffees (from the supermarket sweet aisle)
2 tbsp water
7 Granny Smith apples – each one peeled, cored and cut into 8 wedges
200g (7oz) plain flour
100g (4oz) unsalted butter
100g (4oz) demerara sugar
Ice cream or custard, to serve

1. Preheat the oven to 200°C/180°C Fan/Gas Mark 6. Place the toffees in a saucepan with 2 tbsp of water over a medium heat and stir continuously with a wooden spoon until melted and combined.
2. Add in the apple wedges, coat evenly in the toffee and cook for a few mins before transferring to a baking dish.
3. In a mixing bowl, bring the plain flour, butter and demerara sugar together by rubbing it between your fingertips. Once a crumble consistency is achieved, sprinkle evenly over the top of the toffee apple mixture in the baking dish.
4. Bake for 30 mins until golden and crisp on top. Serve with vanilla ice cream or custard.

EASY PEASY BAKING CAMPAIGN

26	SUNDAY	

27	MONDAY	

28	TUESDAY	

29	WEDNESDAY	*Chinese New Year (Snake)*

30	THURSDAY	

31	FRIDAY	

1	SATURDAY	

CLEVER CLEANING TIPS

Get rid of food odours
Keeping a small bowl filled with bicarbonate of soda powder in your fridge will neutralise odours and keep it smelling fresh. Stir it every few days and replace every two months.

WISE WORDS
'You define your own life. Don't let other people write your script.'
Oprah Winfrey

REMEMBER THIS

'It's for you'
There's nothing new about young people being obsessed with their phones. When we were their age, we were just as bad. There were no mobiles or texting then, just our own voices courtesy of the old Post Office. Sometimes it was school friends, then, later on, boys. We must have driven our parents up the wall!

Recipe of the week

PRAWN CHOW MEIN

SERVES: **2** PREP TIME: **30 mins** COOK TIME: **15 mins**

For the marinade
2 tbsp Lee Kum Kee Gluten Free Light Soy Sauce/Premium Light Soy Sauce, 1 tbsp Lee Kum Kee Pure Sesame Oil, 1 tbsp rice wine, 2 tbsp cornflour

2 tbsp vegetable oil
200g (7oz) prawns
300g (11oz) fresh egg noodles
3 spring onions, trimmed and finely sliced
300g (11oz) beansprouts
3 tbsp Lee Kum Kee Premium Dark Soy Sauce
100g (4oz) basil, finely chopped
Splash of Lee Kum Kee Pure Sesame Oil

1. Mix together the marinade ingredients and marinate the prawns for 15 mins and set aside.
2. Heat a wok over high heat with vegetable oil until it is very hot. Add the prawns and stir-fry for 3 mins. Drain the prawns and set aside.
3. Add noodles, spring onions to wok, stir-fry for 2 mins.
4. Add the beansprouts, Dark Soy Sauce and keep stirring. Add prawns back to the wok and toss.
5. Add the Sesame Oil and basil. Ready to serve.

KEN HOM X LEE KUM KEE

2	SUNDAY

3	MONDAY

4	TUESDAY

5	WEDNESDAY

6	THURSDAY

7	FRIDAY

8	SATURDAY

CLEVER CLEANING TIPS

Get rid of water stains with baby oil

Use baby oil to remove water stains on anything metal or stainless steel. Simply apply a small amount of oil onto a clean cloth, work it directly onto the stain and prepare to be amazed.

WISE WORDS

'In order to be irreplaceable one must always be different.'
Coco Chanel

REMEMBER THIS

Footie fans

Sunday afternoons were about one thing: table football. For a few magical hours every weekend nothing could distract us – not homework, not TV, nothing. Sometimes we would even miss major games being shown on the TV as a result. Hours would go by without us noticing and our wrists would ache afterwards, sometimes for days.

Recipe of the week

BEEF BOURGUIGNON

SERVES: **4** PREP TIME: **10 mins** COOK TIME: **30 mins**

1 packet Idahoan buttery mash
2 tbsp vegetable oil
2 sirloin steaks, fat removed and cut into 2cm cubes
Salt and pepper to season
170g (6oz) smoked bacon lardons
200g (7oz) sliced mushrooms
1 clove garlic, finely chopped
Handful fresh thyme, finely chopped
2 tbsp tomato paste
185ml (7floz) red wine
1 jelly beef stock pot (24g)
1 jar (440g/16oz) sweet silverskin onions

1. Make up the Idahoan mash according to the package instructions and set to one side to cool down. Pour the oil into a heavy-bottomed pot over a medium heat.
2. While the oil heats, dab your steak chunks dry with kitchen paper and season with salt and pepper.
3. Briefly brown the steak chunks – you still want them rare in the middle. Remove and set to one side.
4. Add in the smoked bacon lardons, along with the sliced mushrooms and cook until they start to turn brown before adding in the garlic and thyme.
5. Stir in the tomato paste, then deglaze the pan with red wine. Add the beef stock pot and stir until dissolved.
6. Drain half the vinegar from the onions, then add them to the pan. Simmer, then allow to reduce and thicken.
7. Add in the steak chunks and heat through for a few minutes. Taste and season to your liking. Transfer the mixture to a deep oven dish and heat up the grill.
8. Put the cooled mash into a piping bag and cut a 1cm opening at the tip. Pipe the mash directly on top of the bourguignon in small swirls until the top is covered.
9. Place the whole thing under the grill for 5-10 mins, until the potato has just started to brown slightly.

IDAHOAN PERFECT MASH

9	SUNDAY

10	MONDAY

11	TUESDAY

12	WEDNESDAY

13	THURSDAY

14	FRIDAY	*Valentine's Day*

15	SATURDAY

Dishwashers aren't just for your dishes...

CLEVER CLEANING TIPS

You can use your dishwasher to clean much more than just crockery. Try tossing in your plastic or silicone toys, pet bowls, chew toys and toothbrush holders.

WISE WORDS

'Spread love everywhere you go.'
Mother Teresa

REMEMBER THIS

Mini golf

It was such a silly game. Whole afternoons would seem to fly by in mere moments as we made our slow and steady way around the course, putting carefully over and over again to reach the hole in as few shots as possible. Who cared what the score was though? Sometimes long and enduring friendships would develop out of these games. Sometimes we would even fall in love.

Recipe of the week

RED VELVET COOKIES

SERVES: **8** PREP TIME: **10 mins** COOK TIME: **15 mins**

125g (4oz) unsalted butter
100g (3.5oz) Tate & Lyle Fairtrade Light Brown Sugar
70g (2oz) Lyle's Golden Syrup
1 large egg
5ml (0.18 fl oz) vanilla
5ml (0.18 fl oz) red gel food colouring
260g (9oz) plain flour
10g (0.5oz) cocoa powder
½ tsp baking soda
½ tsp salt
1½ tsp baking powder
200g (7oz) white chocolate chips

1. In a large bowl, cream together the butter, soft light brown sugar, and Lyle's Golden Syrup, until well combined, about 2 mins. Add an egg, vanilla, and the food colouring and mix again to combine.
2. Sift in the flour, cocoa, baking powder, baking soda, and salt and stir to combine with the rest of the ingredients. Lastly, fold in the white chocolate chips. Using a cookie scoop or your hands, scoop the cookie dough and roll it into 6-8 balls (they will be quite big, but feel free to make your cookies smaller, if you prefer), then transfer them onto a baking tray. Place the tray with cookie dough balls into the fridge for 1-2 hours.
3. Once the dough has chilled, preheat the oven to 190°C/170°C Fan/Gas Mark 5. Bake cookies for 12-14 minutes, remove from the oven, and allow them to cool slightly, then transfer to a cooling rack.

TATE AND LYLE SUGARS

16	**SUNDAY**

17	MONDAY

18	TUESDAY

19	WEDNESDAY

20	THURSDAY

21	FRIDAY

22	SATURDAY

CLEVER CLEANING TIPS

Keep your fridge fresh
Lining the salad drawers of your fridge with kitchen towel will make it much easier to remove dirt or food debris in-between cleans. It'll even help keep things like salad leaves fresher for longer.

WISE WORDS

'Love yourself first and everything else falls into line.'
Lucille Ball

REMEMBER THIS?

Hitting the dance floor
Saturday nights were all about dancing. Whether it was the tango, foxtrot, quickstep or something rather more energetic, we lived for those nights throwing some shapes. Nothing else mattered as we twirled and swung around – for a few magical moments, we felt like the centre of the universe. By the end of the night, we'd often feel so dizzy from all the excitement we could barely stand.

Recipe of the week

MOUSSAKA

SERVES: **6** PREP TIME: **10 mins** COOK TIME: **1 hour**

2 aubergines, sliced into discs
1 tbsp vegetable oil
1 onion, diced
1 clove garlic, finely chopped
500g (1lb 2oz) lamb mince
1 tsp ground nutmeg
1 tsp cinnamon powder
2 tsp dried mint
2 tbsp tomato paste
400g (14oz) chopped tomatoes
1 packet Idahoan Buttery Mash
150g (5oz) grated cheese

1. Preheat the oven to 220°C/200°C Fan/Gas Mark 7. In a large pan, fry the aubergine until golden brown, then set aside to drain on a plate lined with kitchen paper.
2. Heat the oil in a heavy-bottomed deep pan and sauté the onion and garlic over a medium heat, until the onion is soft and the garlic starts to caramelise.
3. Add in the lamb mince and brown. Stir in the nutmeg, cinnamon and mint and season. Add the tomato paste and tinned tomatoes and combine.
4. Allow to simmer and reduce slightly before tasting again and seasoning if required.
5. In a deep oven dish, place a layer of aubergine slices, then a layer of mince. Repeat until everything is used.
6. Make the Idahoan Buttery Mash according to the packet instructions and spread evenly on top.
7. Add the grated cheese then place in the oven for 25-30 mins until the topping is golden.
8. Allow the moussaka to rest for a few minutes before serving, so it firms up and is easier to portion.

IDAHOAN PERFECT MASH

23	SUNDAY	

24	MONDAY	

25	TUESDAY	

26	WEDNESDAY	

27	THURSDAY	

28	FRIDAY	*First Day of Ramadan (Islam)*

1	SATURDAY	*St David's Day*

Tackle your keyboard

CLEVER CLEANING TIPS

For those hard-to-reach gaps between the keys on your keyboard, turn the whole thing upside down and tap gently. Use a sticky note folded in half with the glued side facing outwards to tease out stubborn debris.

WISE WORDS

'In a gentle way, you can shake the world.'
Mahatma Gandhi

REMEMBER THIS

The sounds of our youth
We loved our music, in those days. There were no discs or tapes then, it was just records, pure vinyl. We loved the ritual of taking the record out of its sleeve before setting up the player and carefully placing the needle in the right place. We could at least have hummed along to most of the songs in the top 40. These days, we wouldn't have a clue.

Recipe of the week

CHICKEN STEW POT

SERVES: **2** PREP TIME: **5 mins** COOK TIME: **30 mins**

2 x chicken drumsticks
Olive oil
Salt & pepper
½ small onion, diced
½ carrot, diced
1 tsp plain flour
1 beef stock cube
¼ tin of cooked green lentils, drained

1. Pan fry chicken drumsticks for 5 mins over a medium heat in a splash of olive oil along with some salt and pepper.
2. Add onion and carrot and cook for another 7 mins.
3. Add a tablespoon of flour and cook for a further minute before crumbling in a beef stock cube and adding about 200ml of water.
4. Simmer for 15 mins adding tinned green lentils about halfway through. Season to taste.

CAMPANEO

2	SUNDAY	

3	MONDAY	

4	TUESDAY	*Shrove Tuesday (Pancake Day)*

5	WEDNESDAY	*Ash Wednesday*

6	THURSDAY	

7	FRIDAY	

8	SATURDAY	

CLEVER CLEANING TIPS

Unblock your drains

Pour one part baking soda down the drain, then follow it up with two parts white vinegar. Once you see a reaction, wash it down with boiling water. The water will clear away any residue as well as help get rid of pesky drain flies.

WISE WORDS

'If you have good thoughts they will shine out of your face like sunbeams and you will always look lovely.'
Roald Dahl

REMEMBER THIS?

Party time!

Another day, another birthday party. If you were lucky enough to have a party for your big day, it would nearly always be at home. You'd be treated with trifle and orange squash in small paper cups and play games of pass the parcel, musical chairs and pin the tail on the donkey. It was all good fun, though someone would usually have a tantrum by the end.

Recipe of the week

LEMON DRIZZLE SHORTBREAD CRÊPES

SERVES: **4** PREP TIME: **35 mins** COOK TIME: **2 mins**

140g (5oz) plain flour
1 pinch of salt
200ml (7 fl oz) whole milk
100ml (4 fl oz) water
2 eggs
300ml (11 fl oz) whipping cream
300g (11oz) lemon curd
160g (6oz) Walker's Shortbread Fingers
Zest of 1 lemon
30g (1oz) unsalted butter, plus extra to grease the pan

1. Sift the flour into a medium-sized bowl and add the salt. Make a well in the middle of the flour mix.
2. Combine the milk and water. Break the eggs into the well and slowly start whisking. Add the milk and water slowly, whisking constantly until all the flour is combined and the mixture is a smooth batter. Set the batter aside for 30 mins.
3. Lightly whip the cream, gently heat the lemon curd (do not boil) and crumble the Walker's shortbread fingers.
4. After 30 minutes of resting the batter, whisk the lemon zest and melted butter into the batter. Transfer all the batter into a jug for distribution into the pan.
5. Heat a pan over a medium heat. Lightly grease with melted butter. Pour the batter into the pan (around 2 tbsp) and quickly move the pan around so it is evenly coated to the edges with batter. Cook the crêpe for about 45 secs on one side until golden then flip over and cook the other side for about 30-45 secs until golden.
6. Take the crêpe out of the pan, fold twice into a triangle shape and drizzle with warm lemon curd, whipped cream and crumbled shortbread.

WALKER'S SHORTBREAD

9	SUNDAY

10	MONDAY

11	TUESDAY

12	WEDNESDAY

13	THURSDAY

14	FRIDAY

15	SATURDAY

Scrub your cast iron skillet with a potato to lift the dirt

Sprinkle salt onto your pan and, using half a potato, rub the salt around the surface of the pan, buffing out any dirt.

WISE WORDS

'Life is like riding a bicycle. To keep your balance, you must keep moving.'
Albert Einstein

REMEMBER THIS?

Tinkling the ivories

We spent hours and hours having piano lessons and practising. The chords for Happy Birthday, Chopsticks and Baa Baa Black Sheep became so familiar to us after a while that we could practically hear them playing in our sleep. Would it be worth it in the end? Would we fulfil our parents' dreams of achieving musical excellence? We just didn't know.

Recipe of the week

GREEK LAMB WITH ORZO AND APRICOT AND GINGER CHUTNEY

SERVES: **4-6** PREP TIME: **5 mins** COOK TIME: **3 hours**

2 tbsp olive oil
1kg (2lb 3oz) boned shoulder or leg of lamb, cut into 4cm cubes
2 medium onions, sliced
1 tbsp chopped fresh oregano or 1 tsp dried oregano
½ tsp ground cinnamon
400g (14oz) can chopped tomatoes
270g (10oz) jar Tracklements Apricot & Ginger Chutney
500ml (18 fl oz) hot chicken or vegetable stock
400g (14oz) orzo
Freshly grated parmesan, to serve

1. Heat the oven to 180°C/160°C Fan/Gas Mark 4.
2. Add a tbsp of oil to a large, oven- and hob-friendly casserole dish and heat until hot. Brown the lamb, turn the heat down and then add the onions, oregano, ground cinnamon and the rest of the olive oil. Stir well.
3. Pop into the oven uncovered for 45 mins, stirring halfway.
4. Remove from the oven, add the chopped tomatoes, the Apricot & Ginger Chutney and stock, stir then cover tightly and return to the oven for 1.5 hrs, until the lamb is very tender.
5. Stir in the orzo. Cover again and cook for a further 20 mins until the orzo is cooked and the sauce thickened. Stir halfway through.
6. Serve with grated Parmesan, green veg or a mixed salad.

TRACKLEMENTS

16	SUNDAY	

17	MONDAY	*St Patrick's Day (Bank Holiday N. Ireland)*

18	TUESDAY	

19	WEDNESDAY	

20	THURSDAY	

21	FRIDAY	

22	SATURDAY	

CLEVER CLEANING TIPS

Keep your chopping board stain-free

To remove stubborn food stains from plastic chopping boards, try rubbing them with juice from a lemon and leave overnight. Rinse thoroughly or wash on a hot cycle in the dishwasher.

WISE WORDS

'Try to be a rainbow in someone's cloud.'
Maya Angelou

REMEMBER THIS?

Hitting the road

There's nothing quite like the feeling of taking your very first motor car for a drive. The sense of relief and elation you got after passing the driving test opened up your horizons, as you were able to take your car for a spin transporting yourself anywhere you fancied at the drop of a hat. Even simple chores such as dropping in at the petrol station, or washing your car on a Saturday afternoon seemed like special moments to be savoured.

Recipe of the week

PEA & ASPARAGUS FRITTATA

SERVES: **4** PREP TIME: **10 mins** COOK TIME: **10 mins**

125g (4oz) asparagus tips
75g (3oz) frozen peas
6 free-range eggs
100ml (4 fl oz) single cream
25g (1oz) parmesan cheese, grated finely
25g (1oz) butter
4 Padron peppers, halved (or half a small green pepper, deseeded and chopped), optional
125g (4oz) soft goats' cheese

1. Preheat the grill or oven to 160°C/140°C Fan/Gas Mark 3.
2. Bring a small saucepan of salted water to the boil. Add the asparagus and cook for 2 mins. Add the peas and cook for a further 2 mins. Drain and set aside.
3. Whisk the eggs and cream in a large bowl and stir in the grated parmesan.
4. Heat the butter in a non-stick oven proof 20cm (8in) frying pan. Add the Padron peppers and fry for a couple of minutes. Add the asparagus and peas. Stir gently with a wooden spoon then pour in the eggs.
5. Cook over a medium heat for approximately 5 mins until beginning to set around the edges.
6. Dot pieces of goats' cheese evenly around the surface and place under a medium-hot grill (160°C) or oven until golden and just set. Serve warm with dressed salad leaves or cool and cut into wedges for packed lunch.

STELLAR

23	SUNDAY

24	MONDAY

25	TUESDAY

26	WEDNESDAY

27	THURSDAY

28	FRIDAY

29	SATURDAY

DIY descale
Fill your kettle with a mixture of half white vinegar and half water, and leave the kettle unplugged to soak overnight. The next morning, empty the kettle before boiling a fresh kettle-full of water, and rinse thoroughly.

CLEVER CLEANING TIPS

WISE WORDS
'Don't try to lessen yourself for the world; let the world catch up to you.'
Beyoncé

REMEMBER THIS?

Bedtime adventures
We always treasured those final moments before heading to bed and sleep. After a day at school and then playing out in the fresh air, we were physically tired. But now we needed to tire out our overactive imaginations too. And there was no better way to ensure this than by indulging ourselves with a chapter or two of the latest boys' adventure book.

Recipe of the week

WHITE SPELT PISTACHIO AND LIME BUNDT CAKE

MAKES: **1 cake** PREP TIME: **20 mins**   COOK TIME: **45 mins**

Oil for tin
150g (5oz) Doves Farm Organic White Spelt Flour
½ tsp Doves Farm bicarbonate of soda
150g (5oz) pistachios
150g (5oz) butter, chopped into cubes
150g (5oz) caster sugar
3 tbsp finely grated lime rind
2 eggs
2 tbsp milk
2 tbsp lime juice
For the icing: 125g (4oz) icing sugar
2 tbsp lime juice
2 tbsp pistachios, chopped

1. Pre-heat oven to 180°C/160°C Fan/Gas Mark 4. Rub oil on the inside of a metal Bundt tin or silicone mould.
2. Stir flour and soda in a bowl, sieve into another bowl.
3. Put pistachios into a blender, pulse until the size of ground almonds. Put butter into a mixing bowl, add sugar and beat until smooth. Add lime rind.
4. Break eggs into the bowl, one at a time, ensuring each is well incorporated before adding the next. Tip flour into the bowl and stir to combine. Add milk, stir again.
5. Add pistachios and lime juice to bowl and mix well. Tip mixture into Bundt tin or mould, smooth the top.
6. Bake for 40-45 mins or until the sponge springs back when touched. Leave to cool in the tin for 20 mins then turn out onto a wire rack to finish cooling.

For the icing
1. Add icing sugar to a bowl, add some lime juice and stir to combine. Continue adding lime juice and stirring until the icing is just runny enough to pour. Pour icing over the cold cake allowing it to run down the sides.
2. Scatter pistachios over the top. Serve when icing is set.

DOVES FARM

30	SUNDAY	*British Summer Time begins (clocks go forward) & Mothering Sunday*

31	MONDAY

1	TUESDAY

2	WEDNESDAY

3	THURSDAY

4	FRIDAY

5	SATURDAY

CLEVER CLEANING TIPS

Dusting with a sock

Dampen a clean sock with water and run it over your skirting boards or between the slats in your blinds for quick and product-free dusting. Then, simply toss the sock in the wash.

WISE WORDS

'You can cut the flowers but you cannot keep spring from coming.'
Pablo Neruda

REMEMBER THIS?

Making mischief

We used to enjoy a good, old-fashioned pillow fight. Our weapons were soft enough, of course. And one of us could have fallen off the side of the bed or knocked ourselves out on the headboard, but we didn't worry about it. The real sense of danger came from the risk of getting caught.

Recipe of the week

CHICKPEA, CALIFORNIA WALNUT AND POTATO TRAYBAKE

SERVES: **4** PREP TIME: **15 mins** COOK TIME: **55 mins**

700g (1½lb) potatoes, cut into wedges
2 peppers, 1 red, 1 green, thickly sliced
2 tbsp oil
400g (14oz) can chickpeas, drained and rinsed
100g (4oz) frozen sweetcorn, defrosted
150g (5oz) cherry tomatoes, halved
100g (4oz) Cheddar cheese, grated
75g (3oz) California Walnuts
Chopped parsley to garnish

1. Preheat the oven to 220°C/200°C Fan/Gas Mark 7.
2. Place the wedges and peppers on a large baking tray and toss in the oil, season well. Bake for 40 minutes until the potatoes are crispy.
3. Toss in the chickpeas, sweetcorn and tomatoes, then scatter with Cheddar and walnuts. Bake for a further 15 mins until golden. Sprinkle over the parsley to serve.

CALIFORNIA WALNUTS

6	**SUNDAY**

7	MONDAY

8	TUESDAY

9	WEDNESDAY

10	THURSDAY

11	FRIDAY

12	SATURDAY	*First Day of Passover (Jewish Holiday)*

How to clean cloudy glass

CLEVER CLEANING TIPS

If your vase is looking murky, half-fill it with uncooked rice and water. Mix it around to scour the majority of the grime off. Then

pop a dishwasher tablet inside and top it up with hot water. Leave the vase overnight and rinse it out in the morning, leaving you with a sparkling vase.

WISE WORDS

'April hath put a spirit of youth in everything.'
William Shakespeare

REMEMBER THIS

Supermarket sweep

People laugh now, but there was genuine excitement down our way when the first supermarket arrived. First came the countdown to opening and then the cheers when the mayor cut the ribbon. It all seemed so modern and futuristic, and it was great having everything in one place. It was also ideal for catching up on all the local gossip!

Recipe of the week

CHAI LATTE CRUMBLE

SERVES: **2** PREP TIME: **10 mins** COOK TIME: **20 mins**

50g (2oz) plain flour
50g (2oz) porridge oats
150g (5oz) light muscovado sugar
50g (2oz) sunflower seeds
6 heaped tbsp Drink Me Chai Spiced Chai Latte powder
100g (4oz) butter, softened
150g (5oz) walnuts and flaked almonds, roughly chopped
Handful of raisins and sultanas, chopped
1 banana, chopped
300g (11oz) raspberries
300g (11oz) strawberries, hulled and halved
90g (3oz) cherries
125g (4oz) caster sugar
Clotted cream, to serve

1. Preheat the oven to 180°C/160°C Fan/Gas Mark 4
2. Put the flour, oats, sugar, seeds and Drink Me Spiced Chai Latte powder in a mixing bowl. Rub in the butter until evenly distributed and the mixture has formed small clumps with a granola-like look.
3. Spread the mixture evenly over a baking tray. Bake for 20 mins, turning halfway through, or until golden-brown and crisp. Add the chopped nuts and raisins.
4. Place all the fruit in a saucepan with the caster sugar. Bring to a simmer over a medium-low heat and cook, stirring occasionally, until the sugar has dissolved.
5. Spoon the fruit filling on top of your prebaked crumble topping and enjoy with clotted cream.

DRINK ME CHAI

13	**SUNDAY**	*Palm Sunday*

14	MONDAY	

15	TUESDAY	

16	WEDNESDAY	

17	THURSDAY	*Maundy Thursday*

18	FRIDAY	*Good Friday (Bank Holiday)*

19	**SATURDAY**	

CLEVER CLEANING TIPS

Toothpaste can make your iron squeaky clean

Toothpaste isn't only useful when cleaning teeth, it can also make the soleplate of your iron look brand-new. Add a small amount of toothpaste to the bottom of your unplugged, cool iron and, using an old toothbrush, spread the paste in small, circular motions. To remove any excess, use a damp cloth.

WISE WORDS

'For one to have complete satisfaction from flowers, you must have time to spend with them.'
Grace Kelly

REMEMBER THIS

Egg hunts

It was always the best part of Easter. We'd spend a good half hour carefully distributing the eggs around the garden, before the children were unleashed and the Great Easter Egg Hunt would begin. Sometimes the younger ones would need a helpful nod in the right direction. Their cheers of excitement and delight echoed throughout the surrounding woodland.

Recipe of the week

RHUBARB FRANGIPANE TART

SERVES: **8-10** PREP TIME: **40 mins** COOK TIME: **45 mins**

200g (7oz) plain flour
25g (1oz) icing sugar
¼ tsp ground cardamom
⅛ tsp fine salt
105g (4oz) unsalted butter, fridge cold, cut into 1cm cubes
1 large egg yolk, fridge cold
120g (4oz) unsalted butter, room temperature
120g (4oz) golden caster sugar
1 large egg, room temperature
10ml (0.5 fl oz) rum
120g (4oz) ground almonds
¼ orange, zest only
250g (9oz) rhubarb, cut into 3cm sticks on a diagonal
1-2 tbsp demerara sugar
Crème anglaise, whipped cream or ice cream to serve.

1. Mix the flour with the sugar, cardamom and salt in a bowl with a whisk. Add the butter and rub between your fingertips until the mixture resembles coarse sand.
2. Whisk the egg yolk with 1 tbsp of cold water and add to the flour. Mix with a knife, adding another 1 tbsp of cold water if needed to form a dough. Form into a disc, wrap in cling film and allow to rest in the fridge for an hour.
3. Roll out the pastry to the thickness of a pound coin and line an 8in fluted tart tin. Cover once more and rest for 2 hours in the fridge.
4. Preheat the oven to 170°C/150°C Fan/Gas Mark 3. Beat the butter and sugar together until pale and fluffy.
5. Beat in the egg, followed by the rum, almonds and orange zest until smooth.
6. Spoon or pipe the frangipane into your chilled pastry shell and arrange the rhubarb on top – work from the centre and follow the pictured pattern for a chevron effect. Sprinkle it with demerara sugar.
7. Bake on the middle shelf for 35-45 mins or until puffed and set in the centre.Remove and allow to cool.
8. Serve with crème anglaise, whipped cream or ice cream.

STELLAR

| 20 | SUNDAY | *Easter Sunday* |

| 21 | MONDAY | *Easter Monday (Bank Holiday except Scotland)* |

| 22 | TUESDAY | |

| 23 | WEDNESDAY | *St George's Day* |

| 24 | THURSDAY | |

| 25 | FRIDAY | |

| 26 | SATURDAY | |

CLEVER CLEANING TIPS

Freshen up the fridge

Combine one tablespoon of water with two tablespoons of baking soda until it forms a thick paste and spread it onto any areas of discolouration. If you

place a cup of water, baking soda, lemon and essential oils in the fridge, this will also expel any odours.

WISE WORDS

'If you don't like the road you're walking, start paving another one!'
Dolly Parton

REMEMBER THIS

Going out for dinner

Food was generally plainer in those days. Not bad exactly, but certainly less exotic or diverse than it often is today. Eating out anywhere was a rare treat though. We would eat slowly, savouring each mouthful carefully and delicately. Sausages, potatoes, chicken: we loved them all. On very special occasions, we'd even get dessert.

Recipe of the week

PINEAPPLE UPSIDE-DOWN CAKE

SERVES: **6** PREP TIME: **15 mins** COOK TIME: **60 mins**

1 tbsp olive oil, plus some to brush baking pan
200g (7oz) packed light-brown sugar
435g (15oz) tin of Del Monte Pineapple Slices
120g (4oz) all-purpose flour (spooned and levelled)
60g (2oz) whole-wheat flour (spooned and levelled)
1½ tsp baking powder
½ tsp baking soda
½ tsp salt
235ml (8 fl oz) low-fat buttermilk
2 large eggs
1 tsp pure vanilla extract

1. Preheat oven to 180°C/160°C Fan/Gas Mark 4. Brush a 9in square baking pan with oil; line with a strip of parchment paper, leaving an overhang on two sides. Brush paper with oil. Sprinkle bottom of pan with 50g sugar. Arrange the Del Monte pineapple rings in pan.
2. In a medium bowl, whisk together both flours, baking powder, baking soda and salt; then set aside.
3. In a large bowl, whisk together buttermilk, eggs, vanilla extract, oil, and remaining 150g of sugar. Add flour mixture; mix until combined. Pour batter over the pineapple. Tap pan firmly on counter to settle batter, then smooth top.
4. Bake until a toothpick inserted in the centre of the cake comes out clean, this will take 50 to 60 mins.
5. Cool for 20 mins in pan; invert onto a serving platter (peel off and discard paper).

DEL MONTE

27	SUNDAY

28	MONDAY

29	TUESDAY

30	WEDNESDAY

1	THURSDAY

2	FRIDAY

3	SATURDAY

CLEVER CLEANING TIPS

Using lemons to clean your microwave

Place a cup of lemon juice and water in your microwave and let it run for a couple of minutes. This helps to loosen grease and remove any smells. For stubborn stains, try a 50/50 mixture of vinegar and water, or for less stubborn stains, use water and washing-up liquid.

WISE WORDS

'There are always flowers for those who want to see them.'
Henri Matisse

REMEMBER THIS

Fun at the fair

The dodgems were the absolute highlight of the Mayday Spring Fair. We would happily pass up any offers of ice cream or candy floss to ensure we got a place in the driving seat. At first, we would always drive as skilfully as possible, carefully avoiding everyone. Later, we would just try and crash into everything we could!

Recipe of the week

THE ULTIMATE FISH PIE

SERVES: **6** PREP TIME: **40 mins** COOK TIME: **45 mins**

300g (11oz) cod loin
200g (7oz) skinned and boned salmon fillet
175g (6oz) smoked haddock fillet
1 onion, cut into quarters
1 bay leaf
800ml (28fl oz) semi-skimmed milk
80g (3oz) unsalted butter
80g (3oz) plain flour
Large handful of chopped fresh flat-leaf parsley
3 medium eggs
180g (6oz) raw prawns
125g (4oz) frozen garden peas
2 x 109g (4oz) Idahoan Cheddar Cheese Perfect Mash
50g (2oz) mature Cheddar cheese, grated

1. Place the fish into a large pan with onion and bay leaf. Pour over the milk, which should just cover the fish. Place over a medium heat and bring to a simmer. Cook for 1-2 mins, then remove from the heat and gently lift the fish out of the milk and into a bowl. Flake when slightly cooled. Reserve the milk, discarding the bay leaf and onion. Make the milk up to 800ml (28 fl oz).
2. Melt the butter in the pan and stir in the flour. Cook for 1 min over a medium heat, then remove from heat and gradually add the milk, whisking until you have smooth sauce. Place back over the heat and bring to a simmer while stirring, then cook for 2 mins until thickened and smooth. Stir in the parsley and season.
3. Preheat oven to 190°C/170°C Fan/Gas Mark 5. Bring a small pan of water to the boil and cook eggs for 7 mins, drain and run under cold water. Peel off the shells then cut into quarters.
4. Scatter fish into a 1.5-2ltr ovenproof dish, top with prawns, egg and peas. Pour sauce over.
5. Prepare Idahoan Cheddar Cheese Perfect Mash. Spoon mash on top of fish. Sprinkle with the grated Cheddar.
6. Put dish on a baking sheet and cook for 20-30 mins or until bubbling and golden at the edges.

IDAHOAN PERFECT MASH

4	**SUNDAY**	

5	MONDAY	*May Day (Early May Bank Holiday)*

6	TUESDAY	

7	WEDNESDAY	

8	THURSDAY	

9	FRIDAY	

10	SATURDAY	

How to get a sparkling showerhead

If the built-up residue on your showerhead is annoying you, the solution is simple. Tie a bag of vinegar around it, secure with a rubber band, and leave it to soak overnight. In the morning, rinse the showerhead and it'll look brand-new.

WISE WORDS

'It is never too late to be what you might have been.'
George Eliot

REMEMBER THIS

Dining alfresco

Eating outside is a reasonably rare treat for people in this country. Whenever we were on holiday, we would try to do it every day, if we could. Corned beef and cheese sandwiches, ginger cake, apples and lemonade. It didn't really matter what the food was. Somehow everything tasted better simply because we were outside.

Recipe of the week

VEGAN BROWNIES

SERVES: **9-12** PREP TIME: **15 mins** COOK TIME: **45 mins**

150g (5 fl oz) melted vegan dark chocolate
50ml (2 fl oz) melted coconut oil
390ml (14 fl oz) dairy-free milk
90g (3oz) Horlicks Vegan
135g (5oz) plain flour
50g (2oz) coconut flour
80g (3oz) light brown sugar
50g (2oz) cacao powder
1 tbsp ground flaxseed
100g (4oz) vegan white chocolate chunks
50g (2oz) vegan dark chocolate chunks

1. Preheat oven to 180°C/160°C Fan/Gas Mark 4 and grease or line a rectangular baking tin with parchment paper.
2. In a large bowl, combine the melted dark chocolate, melted coconut oil and dairy-free milk. Then add the Horlicks Vegan, plain and coconut flours, light brown sugar, cacao powder and ground flaxseed.
3. Combine well and then fold two-thirds of the white and dark chocolate chunks through the mixture.
4. Pour the mixture into the tin and flatten so it's smooth. Now scatter the remaining chocolate chunks on top and gently push down.
5. Bake in the oven for 40-45 mins or until a toothpick comes out clean.
6. Allow to cool before removing from the tin and serving.

HORLICKS

11	SUNDAY

12	MONDAY

13	TUESDAY

14	WEDNESDAY

15	THURSDAY

16	FRIDAY

17	SATURDAY

Get streak-free windows
When cleaning windows and mirrors, try using balled-up newspaper. It's gentle and won't leave scratches or streaks on the surface.

WISE WORDS
'Wherever life plants you, bloom with grace.'
Unknown

REMEMBER THIS

Sweet shopping
We always felt like proper grown-ups when we were allowed to go to the shop on our own. There was such a rich array of goods available on all the shelves. Usually, we were under orders to get some vital ingredient for that night's meal, perhaps some sugar, salt or salad. But usually, we would be given a little extra money to get a comic or some sweets too.

Recipe of the week

FRUITY CARIBBEAN CHICKEN CURRY

SERVES: **5** PREP TIME: **15 mins** COOK TIME: **20 mins**

1 tbsp vegetable oil
1 onion, chopped
500g (18oz) chicken thigh fillets, diced
1 red pepper, diced
227g (8oz) can pineapple slices, cut into chunks
1 tbsp medium curry powder
400g (14oz) can coconut milk
400g (14oz) can red kidney beans, drained and rinsed
75g (3oz) California Walnuts, roughly chopped
Rice and coriander leaves to garnish

1. Heat the oil in a large frying pan and fry the onion and chicken for 5 mins, add the pepper and pineapple chunks, reserving the juice, and fry for a further 2-3 mins.
2. Stir in the curry powder and cook for 1 min before adding the coconut milk, pineapple juice and kidney beans, simmer for 10 mins then stir in the walnuts, season.
3. Serve with rice garnished with coriander leaves.

CALIFORNIA WALNUT

18	SUNDAY

19	MONDAY

20	TUESDAY

21	WEDNESDAY

22	THURSDAY

23	FRIDAY

24	SATURDAY

CLEVER CLEANING TIPS

Freshen up your sponge!
Kitchen sponges are versatile for cleaning, but they can also spread bacteria. However, if you put a damp sponge in the microwave for 90 seconds on full power, you can reduce the amount of bacteria by a massive 99 per cent.

WISE WORDS

'What you do makes a difference, and you have to decide what kind of difference you want to make.'
Jane Goodall

REMEMBER THIS

Travelling on trams

Most of us never felt any special affection for trams at the time. They were just there, the same as cars, trains and motorbikes. There was always the familiar hum as they moved up and down the street. We assumed they would be there forever. If we had known they were going to disappear one day, we might have used them more often. We all miss them now.

Recipe of the week

ROASTED LEEK, MUSHROOM & GORGONZOLA RIGATONI

SERVES: **2** PREP TIME: **5 mins** COOK TIME: **30 mins**

125g (4oz) leeks, sliced into 1cm rounds
2 tbsp olive oil
160g (7oz) rigatoni
20g (1oz) dried porcini mushrooms
2 garlic cloves, finely sliced
3 tbsp crème fraiche
2 sprigs of fresh thyme, leaves removed
100g (4oz) gorgonzola dolce, crumbled
2 tbsp chopped parsley
Extra virgin olive oil, to serve

1. Preheat the oven to 200°C/180°C Fan/Gas Mark 6. Add the leeks to a baking tray with the olive oil and season well. Toss to combine then roast for 15 mins. Meanwhile, cook the pasta according to the instructions and, once cooked, reserve a mugful of the starchy pasta water.
2. To make the pasta sauce, add the dried porcini mushrooms to a heatproof bowl, pour over 200ml (7 fl oz) of boiling water and leave to soak for 10 mins. Meanwhile place a frying pan on a medium heat and add 1 tbsp of olive oil. Fry the garlic for 5 mins until lightly golden, then lift the soaked mushrooms out of the boiling water and cook for a further 3 mins.
3. Add the cooked pasta to the pan followed by the crème fraiche, thyme leaves, 3 tbsp of pasta water and half the mushroom liquid. Stir continuously over a medium heat until the pasta is coated in the rich creamy sauce. Finally, add the roasted leeks, gorgonzola and chopped parsley, along with another splash of pasta water and mushroom liquor. Season well and make sure the pasta is nice and hot and the gorgonzola has melted, then serve with a drizzle of olive oil on top.

BRITISH LEEKS

25	SUNDAY	

26	MONDAY	*Spring Bank Holiday*

27	TUESDAY	

28	WEDNESDAY	

29	THURSDAY	*Ascension Day*

30	FRIDAY	

31	SATURDAY	

Chalk it up
Use chalk for stubborn grease or oil stains on clothing. Remove any excess grease using a paper towel before covering the area with chalk. For particularly tough stains, add some stain remover before tossing clothes into the wash.

WISE WORDS

'Don't judge each day by the harvest you reap but by the seeds that you plant.'
Robert Louis Stevenson

REMEMBER THIS?

Paddling pools
I suppose you could say we had vivid imaginations. We would spend hours constructing endless sea-based scenarios. Spellbinding stories of ships being attacked by a gigantic octopus or hordes of pirates, or brave explorers marooned in obscure, exotic lands or lured to their doom by hypnotic mermaids. Then the water would get too cold and we would get out.

Recipe of the week

VEGAN BANANA BREAD

SERVES: **10** PREP TIME: **10 mins** COOK TIME: **45 mins**

4 x ripe bananas
75g (3oz) vegetable oil
1 tsp vanilla extract
225g (8oz) wholemeal self-raising flour
2 tsp baking powder
100g (4oz) light brown soft sugar

1. Preheat the oven to 160°C/140°C Fan/Gas Mark 3. Line a loaf tin. Mash 3 of the bananas into a measuring jug with the vegetable oil and vanilla extract.
2. In a mixing bowl, combine the flour, baking powder and sugar. Add the wet mix to the dry mix and combine.
3. Pour into the lined loaf tin and top with the remaining banana, halved lengthways.
4. Bake for 40-45 mins until golden on top and springy to the touch in the centre.

UK FLOUR MILLERS

1	**SUNDAY**

2	MONDAY

3	TUESDAY

4	WEDNESDAY

5	THURSDAY

6	FRIDAY

7	SATURDAY

CLEVER CLEANING TIPS

No extra elbow grease required

To clean your oven, turn the temperature up to a high heat and place an ovenproof bowl full of warm water with some lemon slices inside, and leave for at least 20 minutes.

The steam will loosen any dirt or grime, doing the hard work for you and eliminating the need for extra elbow grease.

WISE WORDS

'Never bend your head. Always hold it high. Look the world straight in the eye.'
Helen Keller

REMEMBER THIS

Mummy's little helper

We always used to enjoy helping mum out in the kitchen. I say 'helping', but I don't know how much help we really were. We certainly made a mess and would end up eating probably more than we actually baked along the way. But we created lots of happy memories, if nothing else.

Recipe of the week

JERSEY ROYAL, GREEN VEGETABLE AND SALMON STEW

SERVES: **4** PREP TIME: **10 mins** COOK TIME: **25 mins**

2 tbsp olive oil
2 shallots, finely chopped
1 small leek, washed and sliced
2 garlic cloves, peeled and crushed
500g (1lb 2oz) Jersey Royal potatoes, scrubbed and cut into pieces if large
100ml (4 fl oz) dry white wine
250ml (9 fl oz) vegetable stock
100ml (4 fl oz) crème fraîche or single cream
4 salmon fillets
125g (4½oz) asparagus tips
100g (4oz) frozen peas
1 small bunch of chives, snipped
1 tsp lemon zest

1. Heat the oil in a sauté pan. Add the shallots, leek and garlic and fry over a low heat until the shallots have softened but not coloured. Add a pinch of salt and freshly ground pepper.
2. Add the Jersey Royal potatoes and pour in the wine. Bring to the boil and cook for 2 mins before adding the stock. Cover the pan with a lid and cook for another 10 mins or until the potatoes are almost cooked.
3. Stir in the crème fraîche or cream and place the salmon fillets in the pan, pressing them down gently. Cover and simmer for 5 mins.
4. Remove the lid, add the asparagus tips and cook for 2-3 mins, then add the peas for the final few minutes of cooking.
5. Divide the stew between 4 bowls, sprinkle with the fresh chives and lemon zest and then serve immediately.

STELLAR

8	SUNDAY

9	MONDAY

10	TUESDAY

11	WEDNESDAY

12	THURSDAY

13	FRIDAY

14	SATURDAY

CLEVER CLEANING TIPS

Use dryer sheets to clean your pans
Leave frying pans or trays in the sink with soap, warm water and a tumble dryer sheet for an hour or two. This will allow you to rinse the grime away.

WISE WORDS

'It is often the small steps, not the giant leaps, that bring about the most lasting change.'
Queen Elizabeth II

REMEMBER THIS

Homemade outfits
We always had to look our very best for the latest dance. Hair, make-up, outfits: everything had to be perfect. Everyone knew you never got a second chance to make a first impression, so we used to devote hours to ensuring we generated the maximum visual impact. The boys never had any idea what we put ourselves through.

Recipe of the week

STIR-FRIED MINCE BEEF WITH GREEN PEAS

SERVES: **4** PREP TIME: **15 mins** COOK TIME: **15 mins**

2 tbsp vegetable oil
1 onion, cut into pieces
400g (14oz) minced beef
Handful fresh coriander
200g (7oz) frozen green peas
4 tbsp Lee Kum Kee Panda Brand Oyster Sauce
3 tbsp Lee Kum Kee Yellow Bean Sauce

1. Heat a wok over high heat with oil until it is very hot. Add the onions and stir-fry them until they become translucent.
2. Add the minced beef and coriander, keep stirring.
3. Add the frozen peas and mix well.
4. Finally add the sauce mixture and simmer for 5 mins. Ready to serve.

KEN HOM X LEE KUM KEE

15	SUNDAY	*Father's Day*

16	MONDAY

17	TUESDAY

18	WEDNESDAY

19	THURSDAY

20	FRIDAY

21	SATURDAY	*Summer Solstice (Longest day)*

De-grime your grout

CLEVER CLEANING TIPS

Make a paste of baking soda and water. Using a toothbrush, work this into the grout between your tiles. Then fill a spray bottle with vinegar and spray it all over the mixture. Continue to scrub this with a toothbrush and finish it up by rinsing the tiles with water.

WISE WORDS

'You're braver than you believe, stronger than you seem, and smarter than you think.'
A.A. Milne

REMEMBER THIS

Lovely lidos

It always took a while to get in. The water seemed so cold, but we were fine once we allowed ourselves to become fully submerged. The strange, eerie, serene, blue unreality of the world underwater. The constant whistle blowing. The feel of the armbands or the white polystyrene floats. The smell of the chlorine. Then, more shivering in the cold again when we got out again.

Recipe of the week

SHORTBREAD CHEESECAKE TRUFFLES

SERVES: **16** PREP TIME: **1hr 30 mins** COOK TIME: **N/A**

150g (5oz) Walker's Shortbread Fingers
150g (5oz) cream cheese
1 tsp vanilla extract
145g (5oz) dark chocolate, melted
1 tbsp coconut oil
Chocolate sprinkles for decoration

1. Finely crush the Walker's Shortbread Fingers.
2. In a separate bowl, combine the cream cheese, vanilla extract and shortbread crumbs.
3. Mix well and chill in the fridge for 20 mins.
4. Remove mix from fridge. Take approximately 1 tbsp of mix, roll into a ball and set on a tray. Continue to create balls until the mix is finished. Chill in the fridge for 30 mins.
5. Melt the chocolate and coconut oil gently. Mix until thoroughly blended, then set aside.
6. Roll each ball in melted chocolate and set on a tray lined with baking paper. Top each ball with the chocolate sprinkles. Refrigerate the truffles for at least 20 mins until the chocolate has set or keep in the fridge until ready to eat!

WALKER'S

22	SUNDAY	

23	MONDAY	

24	TUESDAY	

25	WEDNESDAY	

26	THURSDAY	*Islamic New Year*

27	FRIDAY	

28	SATURDAY	*Armed Forces Day*

Mayo doubles as a gardening tool

CLEVER CLEANING TIPS

Clean dusty potted plants with some soap and warm water, then, using a paper towel, rub a dollop of mayo onto the leaves to make them extra shiny.

WISE WORDS
'It is better to fail in originality than to succeed in imitation.'
Herman Melville

REMEMBER THIS

Perfect picnics
Lardy cake. Cheese sandwiches. Sausage rolls. There was something special about those summer picnics. Maybe it was just the novelty. Dad had just got our first car and we loved the fact that we could be transported to the beauty of the countryside at a moment's notice for the first time. It was wonderful.

Recipe of the week

BREAKFAST PANCAKES WITH BACON AND AVOCADO

SERVES: **6** PREP TIME: **10 mins** COOK TIME: **20 mins**

150g (5oz) self-raising flour
½ tsp cream of tartar
2 tbsp caster sugar
2 large, free-range eggs, separated
125ml (4 fl oz) natural yoghurt
16 rashers streaky bacon
The Groovy Food Company Organic Cooking Spray with Virgin Coconut Oil
2 avocados, sliced
2-3 tbsp The Groovy Food Company Agave Nectar Rich and Dark

1. Sift the flour into a bowl with the cream of tartar and add the caster sugar.
2. Make a well in the centre, add the egg yolks and yoghurt.
3. Mix gradually together to form a thick batter. Set aside while you get the bacon ready.
4. Heat your grill to high and cook the bacon for 5-6 mins, turning until golden and crispy. Set aside under a piece of foil to keep warm.
5. Once bacon is nearly cooked, whip the egg whites in a clean bowl to soft peaks. Fold into the pancake batter.
6. Heat a large non-stick frying pan and spray with a little coconut oil spray, so it forms a very thin layer. Drop heaped tablespoons of the batter into the pan and cook for 2 mins until set and golden on the bottom, then flip over and cook for a further 1-2 mins.
7. Transfer to a plate to keep warm and cook the rest of the pancakes, adding more coconut oil if you need to.
8. Pile up stacks of pancakes scattered with avocado wedges and strips of crispy bacon. Drizzle with the dark agave and serve immediately.

THE GROOVY FOOD COMPANY

29	SUNDAY

30	MONDAY

1	TUESDAY

2	WEDNESDAY

3	THURSDAY

4	FRIDAY	*American Independence Day*

5	SATURDAY

CLEVER CLEANING TIPS

Use tongs to clean your blinds

Wrap the ends of a set of tongs in clean rags and secure with elastic bands. Now grab one slat of the blinds with the tongs and glide along the slats, cleaning the top and bottom simultaneously.

WISE WORDS

'Once you face your fear, nothing is ever as hard as you think.'
Olivia Newton-John

REMEMBER THIS

Wonderful wireless

We would always spend Sunday nights glued to the radio. Whether it was the latest hot songs from the hit parade, a laugh-a-minute comedy show or an 'edge of your seat' drama performance, there was something about the simple pleasure of listening to the wireless that really fired our imaginations. The power of the wireless transfixed us, and nothing on the small black and white flickering screen in the corner of our living room could ever compete with it.

Recipe of the week

TACOS WITH SPICY SPINACH POTATOES AND MINT SAUCE

SERVES: **4** PREP TIME: **10 mins** COOK TIME: **20 mins**

600g (21oz) baby potatoes, halved
2 tbsp olive oil
1 red onion, sliced
3 cloves garlic, sliced
1 tsp cumin seeds
1 tsp turmeric
1 tsp garam masala
300g (10.5oz) cherry tomatoes, chopped
2 tbsp soy sauce
260g (9oz) bag of spinach
4 tbsp vegan yoghurt or mayo
Handful fresh mint, shredded
8 small corn/wheat tacos

1. In a large pan, bring salted water to the boil then add the potatoes. Boil for 10 mins. Drain and set aside.
2. In the meantime, heat the oil in a medium saucepan over a medium heat then add the onion. Fry for 8-10 mins until soft.
3. Now add the garlic and fry for 2-3 mins, stirring frequently.
4. Add the spices and stir to coat everything, then add the tomatoes, soy and allow to cook down for 5 mins.
5. Add the cooked potatoes and spinach and cook for 3 mins and season to taste.
6. To make the mint sauce, mix the yoghurt and shredded mint in a bowl. Season to taste. Cook the tacos according to the instructions on the packet. Load with spiced potatoes and mint sauce.

DISCOVER GREAT VEG

6	SUNDAY

7	MONDAY

8	TUESDAY

9	WEDNESDAY

10	THURSDAY

11	FRIDAY

12	SATURDAY	*Battle of the Boyne*

CLEVER CLEANING TIPS

Hairspray your whiteboard

Dry erase marker stains that won't go away can ruin a whiteboard.

Try spritzing on some hairspray, then wipe down the board with soap and water to get rid of the sticky residue.

WISE WORDS

'In summer, the song sings itself.'
William Carlos Williams

REMEMBER THIS

Setting sail

There was a long build-up, but finally the ship we'd dubbed the HMS Antelope was ready to set sail. We spent days putting it all together and making sure it was watertight, and then had to wait a further week while we waited for the perfect conditions for sailing it. In the end, the maiden voyage was a triumphant success, but for some reason we never did it again.

Recipe of the week

HALLOUMI FLATBREAD WITH TRACKLEMENTS TOMATO & CHILLI CHUTNEY

SERVES: **4** PREP TIME: **15 mins** COOK TIME: **10 mins**

500g (18oz) halloumi, cut into 8 slices
1 clove garlic, crushed
Juice of half a lime plus zest
1 small red cabbage, finely sliced
1 carrot, grated
2 tbsp Greek-style yoghurt
1 tbsp mayonnaise
1 tbsp cider vinegar
½ tsp smoked paprika
4 flatbreads or wraps
1 tbsp olive oil
3 tbsp Tracklements Tomato & Chilli Chutney
Rocket leaves

1. Put the halloumi slices into a shallow bowl and add the crushed garlic, lime juice and zest. Mix well and leave to marinate.
2. Combine the red cabbage and grated carrot into a bowl.
3. Put the yoghurt, mayonnaise, vinegar and smoked paprika into a jug and whisk to a smooth sauce. Pour over the red cabbage and carrot, mix well.
4. Heat the oven to a low temperature and put the flatbreads in to warm.
5. Heat a tbsp of oil in a frying pan over a medium to high heat and fry the halloumi for 3 mins each side until golden.
6. Spread a good dollop of Tracklements Tomato & Chilli Chutney on each flatbread, spoon over some slaw and top with the halloumi and rocket.

TRACKLEMENTS

13	SUNDAY	

14	MONDAY	*Battle of the Boyne (Bank Holiday N. Ireland)*

15	TUESDAY	*St Swithin's Day*

16	WEDNESDAY	

17	THURSDAY	

18	FRIDAY	

19	SATURDAY	

CLEVER CLEANING TIPS

Reuse your candle pots
When a candle is all used up, rinse the container with steaming hot water and scoop out the wax residue with a paper towel. You can then reuse the pot rather than throw it away.

WISE WORDS
'We can't help everyone, but everyone can help someone.'
Ronald Reagan

REMEMBER THIS

Fun and games
There was nothing quite like Sports Day. It was the climax to the school year. The good-natured silliness of the early games: the sack race, three-legged race and the egg and spoon – using real eggs. And who could forget the wheelbarrow race... hilarious! Then finally, the cheers of the crowd got louder as the events grew more serious. The hot sun. Lungs bursting, legs aching, blood pumping, panting furiously, desperately straining to win.

Recipe of the week

CRISPY HALLOUMI TABBOULEH

SERVES: **6** PREP TIME: **15 mins** COOK TIME: **5 mins**

100g (3.5oz) couscous
125ml (4 fl oz) boiling water
1 small red onion, finely chopped
20g (1oz) fresh mint, finely chopped
60g (2oz) flat-leaf parsley, finely chopped
100g (3.5oz) fresh coriander, finely chopped
100g (3.5oz) baby spinach, finely chopped
5cm piece of cucumber, finely chopped
2 salad tomatoes, deseeded and chopped
1 lemon, juiced
2 tbsp olive oil
225g (8oz) pack 30% less fat halloumi
1 tsp sesame seeds
1 tsp plain wholemeal flour
200g (7oz) tub reduced-fat houmous, to serve
Pinch of smoked paprika, to serve (optional)

1. Tip the couscous into a large, heatproof bowl and pour over 125ml (4 fl oz) boiling water; set aside for 5 mins. Put the onion, herbs and spinach in a large mixing bowl with the cucumber, tomatoes, lemon juice and 1 tbsp olive oil; mix well.
2. Fluff up the couscous with a fork and add to the herb mixture. Season to taste and set aside.
3. Cut the halloumi into 8 chunky pieces and pat dry with kitchen paper. In a small bowl, mix together the sesame seeds and flour, then add the halloumi pieces. Heat the remaining oil in a frying pan over a medium-high heat and fry the halloumi for 5 mins, turning frequently, or until golden and crisp all over.
4. Pile the tabbouleh onto a platter and top with the crispy halloumi pieces. Serve with the houmous and sprinkle with smoked paprika, if you like.

TESCO REAL FOOD

20 SUNDAY

21 MONDAY

22 TUESDAY

23 WEDNESDAY

24 THURSDAY

25 FRIDAY

26 SATURDAY

Buff out your floors

CLEVER CLEANING TIPS

You can restore your hardwood floor with a sock or a clean tennis ball – run them over small scuffs to erase the marks. To remove bigger scuffs, add some baking soda to a damp cloth and rub gently. Then rinse any residue with a damp paper towel.

WISE WORDS

'All dreams are within reach. All you have to do is keep moving towards them.'
Viola Davis

REMEMBER THIS?

Garage bands

We weren't the only boys to start our own skiffle band in the mid-Fifties. In fact we were probably not even the only ones in our village! We all dreamed of being the next Lonnie Donegan. Of course we never made it any bigger than playing at the local church fete. But we always received a warm reception from our audiences wherever we went and we had fun along the way.

Recipe of the week

KALE PASTA SAUCE

SERVES: **4** PREP TIME: **10 mins** COOK TIME: **10 mins**

500g (18oz) pasta
1 tbsp olive oil
280g (10oz) kale
3 cloves of garlic, chopped
3 tbsp water
90g (3oz) grated parmesan
240ml (8fl oz) vegetable stock
180g (6oz) cream cheese

1. Cook the pasta according to packet instructions.
2. Meanwhile, in a medium saucepan heat the oil over a medium heat.
3. Add the kale and garlic and fry for about 1-2 mins, until the leaves start to wilt a little, then add the water and keep stirring for a further couple of mins.
4. Transfer the kale and garlic to a food processor and blend for a few minutes then add the grated parmesan, vegetable stock and cream cheese.
5. Blend at full speed until you have a bright green and creamy texture. Stir this in to your cooked pasta then warm through gently before serving. Add a fresh green salad if you like.

DISCOVER GREAT VEG

27	SUNDAY

28	MONDAY

29	TUESDAY

30	WEDNESDAY

31	THURSDAY

1	FRIDAY

2	SATURDAY

Perfect your vacuuming routine

CLEVER CLEANING TIPS

Vacuuming a room horizontally and then vertically helps ensure you get all of the trapped dirt. Vacuuming slowly is also vital to ensure you get every single dirt particle.

WISE WORDS
'The summer night is like a perfection of thought.'
Wallace Stevens

REMEMBER THIS

Carry on camping

Looking back now, it seems amazing that we even managed to do it. All seven of us, cooped up together in such close proximity like that for two weeks. It's impossible to forget now though – the whistle of the kettle, or waking to the noise of the cows mooing in the next field – sounds that will stay with us and trigger special memories forever. Yes, we may have moaned at the time, but of all the holidays in our lives, we definitely enjoyed those ones the best.

Recipe of the week

VEGAN PORRIDGE

SERVES: **3** PREP TIME: **5 mins** COOK TIME: **10 mins**

170g (6oz) porridge oats
50g (2oz) Horlicks Vegan
550ml (19oz) dairy-free milk
Dairy free yoghurt
Peanut butter
Fresh berries
Hazelnuts
Cacao nibs

1. Add the oats, Horlicks Vegan and milk to a pan and cook on a low to medium heat for 10 mins, stirring frequently.
2. Add some more milk should you want a runnier consistency.
3. Top with dairy-free yoghurt, peanut butter, fresh fruit, hazelnuts and cacao nibs, or your usual porridge toppings.

HORLICKS

3	SUNDAY	

4	MONDAY	*Summer Bank Holiday (Scotland)*

5	TUESDAY	

6	WEDNESDAY	

7	THURSDAY	

8	FRIDAY	

9	SATURDAY	

CLEVER CLEANING TIPS

Toothpaste can help with marker stains

If your children have gotten carried away during colouring time, use toothpaste to easily remove marker stains from wood. Apply it lightly with a fingertip and rub in a circular motion, then wipe clean.

WISE WORDS

'A problem is a chance for you to do your best'

Duke Ellington

REMEMBER THIS

Beach days

I mainly remember the searing heat now, looking back. And those sweet, colourful ice lollies, melting in the sun and drooling down our chins. We would sometimes spend whole afternoons building a large sandcastle, and then carefully collect water from the sea in our small plastic buckets and bring it back to fill up the impressive moat we'd dug. The water never seemed to last very long though, instead soaking quickly into the hot sand, leaving the moat damp but empty. We kept ourselves busy, anyway.

Recipe of the week

HERBY FISHCAKES WITH TARTARE SAUCE

SERVES: **3** PREP TIME: **20 mins** COOK TIME: **20 mins**

109g (4oz) pack Idahoan Butter & Herb Perfect Mash
300g (10.5oz) tinned salmon or tuna, or leftover cooked fish, flaked (we used salmon and cod)
200g (7oz) plain flour
Large handful of fresh flat-leaf parsley, chopped
2 tbsp olive oil
5 tbsp mayonnaise, or crème fraîche, for a lighter option
1 tsp capers, chopped
1 spring onion or small shallot, chopped
1 tsp lemon juice
1 lemon, quartered
100g (3.5oz) watercress leaves

1. Prepare your Idahoan Butter & Herb Perfect Mash to packet instructions. Gently mix together with the fish, 150g (5oz) flour and the chopped parsley. Season with salt and pepper. Chill in the fridge for 1 hour 30 mins. Then add the remaining flour and shape into 6 patties.
2. Mix the mayonnaise, capers, parsley, onion and lemon juice to make the tartare sauce and season with salt and pepper. Leave in the fridge until using.
3. Heat the oil in a large frying pan and cook fishcakes for 8 mins, turning once, until they are golden and crispy on the outside. Serve with sauce, a wedge of lemon and some watercress.

IDAHOAN PERFECT MASH

10	SUNDAY

11	MONDAY

12	TUESDAY

13	WEDNESDAY

14	THURSDAY

15	FRIDAY

16	SATURDAY

Tackle stubborn oven grime with a dishwasher tablet

Wearing rubber gloves, dip a dishwasher tablet into a bowl of hot water, and then use the flat side of the tablet to tackle baked-on food and other build-ups in your oven.

WISE WORDS

'The Sun himself is weak when he first rises, and gathers strength and courage as the day gets on.'
Charles Dickens

REMEMBER THIS

Our own little plot

After all those years growing up in the flat, we couldn't believe our luck when our new house came with its own small back garden. It was marvellous. Not only was there enough room for our own paddling pool, and for the cat to wander around, but there was the opportunity to have so much fun in the open air.

Recipe of the week

LEMON CURD DOUGHNUTS

SERVES: **8** PREP TIME: **20 mins** COOK TIME: **10 mins**

150ml (5 fl oz) warm water
70ml (2 fl oz) warm milk
1 sachet fast-action yeast
20g (1oz) caster sugar plus extra for dusting
375g (13oz) plain flour
30ml (1 fl oz) vegetable oil plus extra for shallow frying
2 tsp baking powder
Pinch of salt
Jar of lemon curd

1. In a large mixing bowl, combine the warm water, warm milk, yeast, sugar and a third of the flour. Cover with a tea towel and leave to prove for 10 mins – use this time to heat your oil for frying in the pan or deep fat fryer to 185°C.
2. After the 10 mins, mix the 30ml (1 fl oz) oil, baking powder and salt into the yeast mixture before adding the remaining flour and bringing it together by hand to form a sticky dough.
3. Tip the dough out onto a lightly floured surface and sprinkle some flour on top of the dough, then roll out to a thickness of 2cm.
4. Cut out the doughnuts using a glass or a cutter, then carefully transfer to the hot oil 2-3 at a time, dipping away from you as you put them in.
5. Let the doughnuts cook for 2-3 mins on one side until golden brown, then use the wooden spoon to flip them over and cook for a further 2-3 mins.
6. Remove the doughnuts from the oil and drain them on some paper towels before rolling them in the caster sugar to generously coat the outside of the doughnuts.
7. When all of the doughnuts have been cooked, sugar-dusted and cooled slightly, use the end of the wooden spoon to poke a hole at the top of each doughnut.
8. Fill the doughnuts with the lemon curd, using a piping bag or the corner of a sandwich bag, or carefully tease it in with a teaspoon.

EASY PEASY BAKING CAMPAIGN

17 SUNDAY

18 MONDAY

19 TUESDAY

20 WEDNESDAY

21 THURSDAY

22 FRIDAY

23 SATURDAY

CLEVER CLEANING TIPS

Soften your towels without fabric softener

Ditch the fabric softener as it can actually harden towels. Instead, wash your towels with 250ml of white vinegar, then again with half a cup of baking powder. You can also add a few drops of essential oil for an added element of luxury.

WISE WORDS

'The most difficult thing is the decision to act; the rest is merely tenacity.'
Amelia Earhart

REMEMBER THIS

The great British seaside

There's nothing like the first day of the holiday. The routine would always be the same. We would arrive and drop off our suitcases at the B&B and then embark on the obligatory stroll round the area. I'll always remember the hustle and bustle, the sounds of the Punch and Judy man coming from the beach, the smell of fish and chips and the salty sea air.

Recipe of the week

TUNA SWEET POTATO JACKET WITH MANGO AND RED ONION SALSA

SERVES: **2** PREP TIME: **10 mins** COOK TIME: **12 mins**

2 x 110g (4oz) cans Princes Drained Tuna Steak in Spring Water
2 sweet potatoes, scrubbed
1 small ripe mango, pitted, peeled and finely chopped
½ red or green chilli, deseeded and finely chopped
¼ cucumber, finely chopped
½ red onion, finely chopped
1 tbsp fresh parsley, finely chopped
Salt and freshly ground black pepper
Squeeze of lime or lemon juice

1. Tip the cans of tuna onto a plate and break into chunks. Set aside.
2. To microwave the sweet potatoes, allow 10-12 mins on full power. Ensure sweet potatoes are piping hot throughout.
3. Meanwhile, mix together the mango, chilli, cucumber, red onion and parsley. Season.
4. Fill the sweet potatoes with the mango salsa and top with the tuna chunks. Add a squeeze of lime or lemon juice, then serve.

PRINCES FISH

24	SUNDAY	

25	MONDAY	*Summer Bank Holiday (Except Scotland)*

26	TUESDAY	

27	WEDNESDAY	

28	THURSDAY	

29	FRIDAY	

30	SATURDAY	

CLEVER CLEANING TIPS

Keep your linens smelling fresh

Leaving an open bowl of baking soda near your sheets and towels can help prevent a dank smell. So pop one in your linen closet and replace it regularly.

WISE WORDS

'Where there's hope, there's life.'
Anne Frank

REMEMBER THIS

Bathing beauties

On a day trip to the beach in summer with our closest girlfriends, we felt like Amazon queens. Young, beautiful and headstrong, we thought we could do anything and we were ready to take on the world. Everyone should have the opportunity to feel like that at some point in their lives. We certainly got plenty of attention from all the boys down on the beach and, quite frankly, we loved every last minute of it!

Recipe of the week

CAVOLO NERO FALAFELS WITH HARISSA YOGHURT SAUCE

SERVES: **2** PREP TIME: **10 mins** COOK TIME: **10 mins**

400g (14oz) can chickpeas, drained and rinsed
200g (7oz) cavolo nero, thick stalks removed
1 tbsp tahini
1 clove garlic
½ tsp ground cumin
½ tsp ground coriander
2 tbsp vegetable oil
100g (3.5oz) yoghurt alternative
1 tsp harissa paste

1. Place the chickpeas in a food processor with the leaves from 2 stems of cavolo nero, roughly chopped, the tahini, garlic and spices and blend to a coarse paste. Season well, divide into eight and roll into balls.
2. Heat the oil and fry the falafels for 2-3 mins until golden, turning once halfway. Remove and add the remaining cavolo nero, shredded, and fry for 2-3 mins. Season to taste.
3. Meanwhile, mix together the yoghurt and harissa. Serve the falafels on top of the cavolo nero and drizzle with the harissa yoghurt.

DISCOVER GREAT VEG

31	SUNDAY

1	MONDAY

2	TUESDAY

3	WEDNESDAY

4	THURSDAY

5	FRIDAY

6	SATURDAY

CLEVER CLEANING TIPS

Vegetable oil keeps floors shining

If your wood floors are looking a bit dull, you don't need to use expensive polishers. Just combine equal parts vegetable oil and white vinegar in a spray bottle, spritz the floor, and then mop up the solution.

WISE WORDS

'The most wasted of days is one without laughter.'
E.E. Cummings

REMEMBER THIS

Holidays with friends

There was nothing better than being able to take a friend with you on a family holiday. We laughed such a lot in those days, especially when we were on holiday. We set ourselves off sometimes, often giggling away together at virtually nothing. And it was a bonus for our parents as they were able to enjoy a bit peace and quiet while we had a partner in crime!

Recipe of the week

WILD GARLIC PESTO TAGLIATELLE

SERVES: **4** PREP TIME: **15 mins** COOK TIME: **15 mins**

100g (4oz) wild garlic leaves, washed and patted dry (when garlic not in season, use rocket leaves and basil)
50g (2oz) parmesan cheese, grated finely
50g (2oz) toasted pine nuts (or toasted hazelnuts), plus extra for serving
Olive oil (or rapeseed oil)
Small lemon
300g (10.5oz) tagliatelle
Grated parmesan to serve

1. Roughly chop the wild garlic leaves.
2. Place the wild garlic leaves, parmesan and pine nuts in a food processor and blitz to form a rough paste.
3. With the motor running slowly, add olive oil until you have a loose purée. Add a squeeze of lemon juice, to taste.
4. Use a spatula to transfer the pesto into a small bowl or jar.
5. Bring a large saucepan of salted water to a boil.
6. Cook the pasta according to pack instructions, drain and toss with the pesto.
7. Serve with extra parmesan and pine nuts.

STELLAR

7	**SUNDAY**

8	MONDAY

9	TUESDAY

10	WEDNESDAY

11	THURSDAY

12	FRIDAY

13	**SATURDAY**

CLEVER CLEANING TIPS

Get rid of bacteria on phones or bags

Think of how often your phone and bag are exposed to bacteria when you go out. Give them a quick clean every time you come home with a disinfectant wipe.

WISE WORDS

'It isn't where you came from. It's where you're going that counts.'

Ella Fitzgerald

REMEMBER THIS

Secretarial college

After leaving school, we entered the real world. Surely there was more to life than this? The monotonous clickety click of typists and the dictation seemed unbearable. Some of us even started to miss the familiar certainties of school.

Recipe of the week

PLUM AND ROSEMARY SOURDOUGH FOCACCIA

MAKES: **1 loaf** PREP TIME. **20 mins (plus stretching, folding and overnight proving)** COOK TIME: **25 mins**

100g (3.5oz) sourdough starter
380ml (13 fl oz) warm water
1 tbsp olive oil
2 tsp salt
500g (18oz) strong white bread flour
Sea salt
3-4 ripe plums, stones removed and cut into quarters
Fresh rosemary leaves
2-3 tbsp extra virgin olive oil

1. Place the starter, water and oil in a large mixing bowl and whisk until the mixture is frothy. Stir in the salt.
2. Add flour and stir to form a loose dough.
3. Transfer dough to a large lightly oiled bowl or plastic container and cover. Rest at room temp for 30 mins.
4. Using slightly wet or oiled hands, stretch and fold the dough. Repeat this every 30 mins for 2 hours.
5. Keep the dough covered for 4 hours in a warm room until it forms air bubbles and has increased in bulk. Place covered dough in the fridge overnight.
6. The next day, pour 2-3 tbsp of oil into large frying pan.
7. Using oiled hands gently tip dough into centre of pan. Fold one side of dough towards the centre then repeat on the other side creating a seam in the middle. Turn over so seam is at the bottom with the smooth side up. Stretch very gently to cover the surface of the pan.
8. Cover dough loosely with upturned bowl. Leave at room temp for 2-3 hours until bubbly and increased in bulk.
9. Preheat oven to 220°C/200°C Fan/Gas Mark 7. Drizzle oil on dough, then dimple by pressing with fingers.
10. Top dough with salt. Press plums into the dough and sprinkle with rosemary. Bake for 25 mins until golden.
11. Remove from oven and let it rest for a minute or so and then transfer to a cooling rack. Drizzle with extra virgin olive oil and serve.

STELLAR

14	SUNDAY

15	MONDAY

16	TUESDAY

17	WEDNESDAY

18	THURSDAY

19	FRIDAY

20	SATURDAY

CLEVER CLEANING TIPS

Washing-up liquid isn't just for dishes

Mix some warm water and washing-up liquid and use it to wipe down your patio tables and chairs, then give them a rinse with your garden hose.

WISE WORDS

'If I cannot do great things, I can do small things in a great way.'
Martin Luther King Jr.

REMEMBER THIS

Trip to the zoo

We all had our favourite bits. Dad loved seeing the big beasts like the lions or the elephants, Mum liked anything in water, we marvelled at the multicoloured birds, while our little brothers loved seeing the antics of the chimpanzees in the monkey house. Trips to the zoo with the family were fun treats we looked forward to.

Recipe of the week

TURKEY MEATBALLS WITH HERBED ORZO AND A GREEK SALAD

SERVES: **4** PREP TIME: **15 mins** COOK TIME: **30 mins**

454g (16oz) lean ground turkey
75g (3oz) feta cheese
40g (1oz) oats or panko breadcrumbs
3 tbsp fresh oregano, chopped and divided
3 tbsp fresh dill, chopped and divided
2 tbsp fresh mint, chopped
2 tbsp minced shallot
1 tbsp minced garlic
1½ tsp salt, divided
1½ tsp ground black pepper
720ml (25 fl oz) water
227g (8oz) orzo
Small red onion sliced
1 tbsp lemon zest
3 tbsp chopped sun-dried tomatoes
Garnish: halved tomatoes (optional)

1. Preheat the oven to 175°C/150°C Fan/Gas Mark 3 and line a rimmed baking sheet with foil.
2. In a large bowl, stir together turkey, feta, oats or breadcrumbs, 2 tbsp each oregano and dill, mint, shallot, garlic, ½ tsp salt and pepper. Divide mixture and shape into 12 meatballs. Place on a prepared pan. Bake for 25 mins.
3. Meanwhile, in a medium saucepan, bring water to boil over medium-high heat. Add orzo and remaining salt and cook for 5 mins or just until tender; drain. Transfer orzo to a medium bowl, and stir in onion, lemon zest, sun-dried tomatoes, and remaining 1 tbsp each oregano and dill. Garnish with fresh tomatoes as desired.
4. Serve with a simple salad of chopped tomatoes, cucumber, olives, red onion and Greek dressing.

LINGO

21	SUNDAY	

22	MONDAY	*Jewish New Year (Rosh Hashanah)*

23	TUESDAY	

24	WEDNESDAY	

25	THURSDAY	

26	FRIDAY	

27	SATURDAY	

CLEVER CLEANING TIPS

Get rid of pesky stains on your carpet

Sprinkle baking soda onto the stain, then place a damp paper towel on top and leave it alone for about three hours. Then simply remove the towel and vacuum up any residue. For any stubborn greasy stains, dab some washing-up liquid onto the area and press with a damp towel, then repeat the process.

WISE WORDS

'Life isn't about finding yourself. Life is about creating yourself.'
George Bernard Shaw

REMEMBER THIS

Cuddly companions

It didn't really matter if it was Mollie the dog, Barnaby the rabbit or even Ella the elephant, we always slept best when we had a little cuddly toy resting loyally by our side. Utterly serene and in a perfect state of harmony and absolute comfort, we wouldn't have been woken by a hurricane.

Recipe of the week

BAKED LEEKS WITH HAM & CALIFORNIA WALNUT RATATOUILLE

SERVES: **4** PREP TIME: **15 mins** COOK TIME: **25 mins**

2 large leeks, trimmed, each cut into 4
2 x 375g (13oz) cans ratatouille
150g (5oz) orzo pasta
75g (3oz) California Walnuts, roughly chopped
½ x 25g (1oz) pack basil, shredded
130g (5oz)/4 slices honey roast ham, diced
50g (2oz) mature Cheddar cheese, grated

1. Preheat the oven to 200°C/180°C Fan/Gas Mark 6.
2. Blanch the leeks in boiling, salted water for 2-3 mins until just tender, drain.
3. Heat the ratatouille in a medium saucepan with half a can of water until just boiling. Add the orzo, half the walnuts and the basil, season and transfer to a 2 litre serving dish and bake for 15 mins.
4. Stir in the ham and nestle in the leeks. Scatter over the cheese and remaining walnuts and bake for a further 10 mins.

CALIFORNIA WALNUT

28	SUNDAY

29	MONDAY

30	TUESDAY

1	WEDNESDAY

2	THURSDAY

3	FRIDAY

4	SATURDAY

CLEVER CLEANING TIPS

Getting rid of coffee stains

Want to have a cup of coffee or tea in the morning but your mug looks a bit stained? No problem! Squirt some washing-up liquid in it and add some baking soda, then clean as usual.

WISE WORDS

'The purpose of our lives is to be happy.'
Dalai Lama

REMEMBER THIS

Beloved Bunty

We couldn't wait until Tuesday when the latest issue of Bunty would be published. Tales of Tarzan-like girls who had been raised by wolves sat alongside the adventures of a teenage ballerina and those of four boarding school girls all called Mary. For one glorious hour every week, we would be completely absorbed and totally silent.

Recipe of the week

SHEPHERD'S PIE

SERVES: **6** PREP TIME: **30 mins** COOK TIME: **1 hour**

1 tbsp olive oil
1 large onion, chopped
2 carrots, peeled and chopped
1 garlic clove, chopped
2 stalks rosemary, leaves picked and chopped
4 tinned anchovy fillets, chopped (optional)
500g (18oz) lamb mince (or vegetarian alternative)
2 tbsp tomato purée
400ml (14 fl oz) stock
1 tbsp Worcestershire sauce
150g (5oz) frozen garden peas
2 x 109g (4oz) Idahoan Buttery Perfect Mash

1. Heat the oil in a large saucepan and cook the onion and carrots over a medium heat for 10 mins, adding the garlic for the last couple of minutes.
2. Stir in the rosemary and anchovies and cook for a further 5 mins. Add the mince and stir until cooked, then add in the tomato purée and stock.
3. Bring to a gentle simmer, add the Worcestershire sauce and cook for 20 mins until thickened. Stir in the peas and spoon into a 1.25 litre ovenproof dish.
4. Preheat the oven to 200°C/180°C Fan/Gas Mark 6. Prepare the Idahoan Buttery Perfect Mash to packet instructions. Spoon the mash over the top of the mince, place on a baking tray and cook for 30 mins.

IDAHOAN PERFECT MASH

5	SUNDAY

6	MONDAY

7	TUESDAY

8	WEDNESDAY

9	THURSDAY

10	FRIDAY

11	SATURDAY

Cut the cost of carpet cleaning

CLEVER CLEANING TIPS

Did you know that shaving foam is great for cleaning carpets? Simply squirt a bit over a stain, give it a good rub and wipe away the foam for great results! A basic shaving foam will work out much cheaper than carpet cleaning spray.

WISE WORDS
'Autumn is a second spring when every leaf is a flower.'
Albert Camus

REMEMBER THIS?

Going round in circles
We almost wore the hula hoops out some years. We couldn't get enough of them. Sometimes we would borrow a stopwatch and take turns seeing who could hula for the longest. Sometimes we'd try to race them along the ground or make up stories based around the hoops. It was a great time.

Recipe of the week

NO KNEAD AIR FRYER BREAD

SERVES: **6** PREP TIME: **1 hour 30 mins** COOK TIME: **50 mins**

1 packet (7g) fast-action yeast
480g (17oz) wholemeal bread flour
120g (4oz) high-fibre seed mix
1 tsp salt
480ml (17fl oz) warm water

1. Combine the yeast, wholemeal flour, mixed seeds (keeping 30g/1oz for later) and salt in a large mixing bowl. Add the warm water and bring everything together to form a sticky dough. Cover with a damp cloth and leave to rise in a warm place for at least one hour.
2. Once the dough has doubled in size, tip it out onto a lightly floured surface, deflate the dough by punching out the air, sprinkle more flour on top and shape it into a ball before placing it into a lined cake tin.
3. Score the top, sprinkle with the remaining seed mix, re-cover with the damp cloth and leave to rise for 10-15 mins. Preheat your air fryer to 200°C in the meantime.
4. Cover the dough lightly with aluminium foil and place the whole thing in the air fryer and bake for 30 mins. Then remove the foil from the top and continue to bake the bread for a further 15-20 mins until it is golden on top.
5. Carefully remove the bread from the air fryer and the tin, and allow to cool completely before slicing and serving.

UK FLOUR MILLERS

12	SUNDAY

13	MONDAY

14	TUESDAY

15	WEDNESDAY

16	THURSDAY

17	FRIDAY

18	SATURDAY

CLEVER CLEANING TIPS

Unscratch your plates with baking soda

Combine baking soda with some warm water and spread the paste onto any crockery with scratch marks, then rinse and clean as normal.

Baking Soda

WISE WORDS
'Lead from the heart, not the head.'
Princess Diana

REMEMBER THIS?

Bathing by the fire
It seems barmy to admit it now, but some of the best baths we ever had were taken in that little tin bath. Sometimes it would be placed by the fire in the front room. We would take turns, each of us sharing the water of our siblings. When our time came, none of us ever wanted to get out.

Recipe of the week

SPICED STICKY TOFFEE SANDWICH CAKE

SERVES: **12** PREP TIME: **30 mins** COOK TIME: **45 mins**

330g (11.5oz) unsalted butter, softened, plus extra for greasing
150g (5oz) date syrup
½ tsp ground cinnamon
½ tsp mixed spice
1 tsp bicarbonate of soda
225g (8oz) light brown soft sugar
4 large eggs
325g (11.5oz) self-raising flour
½ tbsp vanilla extract
4 tbsp dulce de leche
90g (3oz) soft cheese
300g (10.5oz) icing sugar, sifted

1. Preheat oven to 180°C/160°C Fan/Gas Mark 4. Grease and line the bases of 2 x 20cm loose-based cake tins.
2. Put the date syrup in a pan on a gentle heat. Stir in cinnamon, spice, soda and a pinch of sea salt until warmed through and combined. Set aside for 5 mins.
3. In a large mixing bowl beat 180g (6oz) butter and brown sugar, until pale and creamy. Beat in the eggs one at a time, then stir in the flour, vanilla and date syrup mixture. When smooth, divide between tins and bake for 35-45 mins, until a skewer inserted comes out clean.
4. Leave cakes in the tins for 10 mins, then turn out dome-side up onto a cooling rack. Spread the top of one of the cakes with 2 tbsp dulce de leche then let them cool.
5. Beat remaining butter with the soft cheese and icing sugar for 3-4 mins, until creamy. Spread half the buttercream on untopped cake. Drizzle or dollop over 2 tbsp dulce de leche, swirling it around so it drizzles down the side a little, then top with the other cake.
6. Spoon remaining icing over the top cake and use the back of a spoon to create swirls. Drizzle over the remaining dulce de leche before serving.

THE GROOVY FOOD COMPANY

19	SUNDAY	

20	MONDAY	*Diwali (Hindu Festival)*

21	TUESDAY	*Trafalgar Day*

22	WEDNESDAY	

23	THURSDAY	

24	FRIDAY	

25	SATURDAY	

CLEVER
CLEANING
TIPS

Get a lemon-fresh sink

Peel a lemon and put the rinds down the disposal (make sure they're small enough not to block your sink). Then run the cold water to get rid of any sour odours.

WISE WORDS

'I'm so glad I live in a world where there are Octobers.'
Anne of Green Gables

REMEMBER THIS?

Feline friends

There's always been something about cats. Maybe it's their free and independent nature and spirit. Their apparent innocence, never-ending sense of curiosity, but also their capacity to be vicious and cruel. They are a mass of contradictions. No two cats are the same and yet not one cat seems simple and straightforward. They are amazing creatures.

Recipe of the week

CALIFORNIA WALNUT AND VEGETABLE PASTA BAKE

SERVES: **4** PREP TIME: **15 mins** COOK TIME: **20 mins**

250g (9oz) macaroni
2 x 400g (14oz) cans minestrone soup
400g (14oz) can borlotti beans, drained and rinsed
100g (3.5oz) frozen peas
75g (3oz) California Walnuts, roughly chopped
50g (2oz) breadcrumbs
50g (2oz) mature Cheddar cheese, grated

1. Preheat the oven to 200°C/180°C Fan/Gas Mark 6.
2. Cook the macaroni in boiling salted water for 7 mins, drain and return to the pan. Add in the soup together with half a can of water, the borlotti beans, peas and 50g walnuts. Bring to the boil and season.
3. Transfer the mixture to a 2-litre serving dish. Combine the breadcrumbs, cheese and remaining walnuts and sprinkle over the pasta. Bake in the oven for 20 mins until golden.

CALIFORNIA WALNUT

| 26 | SUNDAY | *British Summer Time ends (clocks go back)* |

| 27 | MONDAY |

| 28 | TUESDAY |

| 29 | WEDNESDAY |

| 30 | THURSDAY |

| 31 | FRIDAY | *Halloween* |

| 1 | SATURDAY | *All Saints' Day* |

Steam away the grease

CLEVER CLEANING TIPS

A steamer isn't just handy for wrinkly clothes, they can be used to remove grime and dirt from stovetops and kitchen cabinets.

WISE WORDS

'Every day may not be good, but there is something good in every day.'
Unknown

REMEMBER THIS?

Hospital heroes

Being sick was obviously far from ideal but when it was time to leave hospital, we had all developed strong ties to the assorted group of nurses and doctors assigned to look after us. Feeding us, checking our temperature, bathing us, helping us to get better: they'll live on in our hearts and in our memories forever.

Recipe of the week

PUMPKIN SPICE MUFFINS

SERVES: **12** PREP TIME: **10 mins** COOK TIME: **30 mins**

215g (7.5oz) pumpkin purée (this comes in a can and is available in supermarkets)
2 eggs
125ml (4 fl oz) sunflower or vegetable oil
75ml (3 fl oz) water
300g (11oz) caster sugar
225g (8oz) self-raising flour
1 tsp bicarbonate of soda
3 tsp mixed spice
Pumpkin seeds

1. Preheat the oven to 180°C/160°C Fan/Gas Mark 4.
2. In a large mixing bowl, whisk together the pumpkin purée, eggs, oil and water then add in the sugar, flour, bicarbonate of soda and mixed spice and whisk until a smooth batter is formed.
3. Divide the batter evenly between muffin cases, top with a sprinkling of pumpkin seeds and bake for 25-30 mins until risen, golden and springy to the touch. Allow to cool before serving.

EASY PEASY BAKING CAMPAIGN

2	SUNDAY

3	MONDAY

4	TUESDAY

5	WEDNESDAY	*Guy Fawkes Night*

6	THURSDAY

7	FRIDAY

8	SATURDAY

Freshen up your bin with a cotton ball

CLEVER CLEANING TIPS

Take a cotton ball and soak it in essential oil. Drop this in your bin underneath your liner and you've got a simple and inexpensive odour repellent.

WISE WORDS

'Autumn shows us how beautiful it is to let things go.'
Unknown

REMEMBER THIS

School's out!

The best days of your life? We certainly didn't believe that. School wasn't all bad but it wasn't always great either. We would sit for hours, hunched over our desks, surreptitiously looking up at the clock every few seconds as it made its slow journey towards four o'clock, yearning to be free again.

Recipe of the week

TOFFEE APPLE BANGER HOT DOGS

SERVES: **4** PREP TIME: **10 mins** COOK TIME: **30 mins**

8 sausages
½ red onion, finely sliced
¼ small red cabbage, finely sliced
1 Gala apple, or similar red-skinned apple, finely sliced
1 red chilli, finely chopped (optional)
2 tbsp natural or Greek-style yoghurt
1 tbsp mayonnaise
5 tsp honey
1 tsp sriracha sauce, plus extra to serve (optional)
4 Tesco Finest brioche hot dog rolls

1. Preheat the oven to 220°C/200°C Fan/Gas Mark 7. Line a baking tray or roasting tin with greaseproof paper and lay out the sausages. Roast for 30 mins, turning the sausages halfway, until cooked through.
2. Put the red onion, cabbage, apple and half the chilli (if using) in a bowl, then mix in the yoghurt and mayonnaise. Season to taste and set aside.
3. In a small bowl mix together the honey, sriracha sauce and the other half of fresh chilli. When the sausages have roasted for 20 mins, use a pastry brush or spoon to liberally glaze the sausages with the honey mix. Return to the oven for 5-10 mins until they're nice and sticky.
4. To serve, slice into each hot dog roll and stuff with some coleslaw, then top with a sticky sausage and brush with any remaining honey. Drizzle with sriracha if you like an extra kick!

TESCO REAL FOOD

9	**SUNDAY**	*Remembrance Sunday*

10	MONDAY

11	TUESDAY

12	WEDNESDAY

13	THURSDAY

14	FRIDAY

15	SATURDAY

CLEVER CLEANING TIPS

Use flour for a kitchen sink shine

If you have a stainless-steel sink, you'd be surprised how effective flour can be. Wash and dry the sink as normal, sprinkle it with flour, and then get buffing.

WISE WORDS

'You can't go back and change the beginning, but you can start where you are and change the ending.'
C.S. Lewis

REMEMBER THIS

Pogo sticks

Simple toys were always the best. Thanks to space hoppers, inflatable castles, school sack races and pogo sticks, we did a lot of jumping around in those days. Sometimes we would just spin around and around endlessly until we couldn't walk anywhere without falling over. Pogoing was different. Like skateboarding, it took a certain amount of skill and practice.

Recipe of the week

SAUSAGE AND GRAIN STIR FRY

SERVES: **2** PREP TIME: **15 mins** COOK TIME: **20 mins**

175g (6oz) frozen mixed vegetables, defrosted
75g (3oz) California Walnuts
3 reduced fat pork sausages
2 tbsp olive oil
200g (7oz) cherry tomatoes, halved
250g (9oz) pouch mixed grains
100g (3.5oz) spinach
150g (5oz) fat-free natural yoghurt
2 tsp wholegrain mustard

1. Place the mixed vegetables and half the walnuts in a food processor and pulse to give a coarse paste. Remove the skins from the sausages and mix the meat into the vegetable paste and season. Divide into 20 small balls.
2. Heat the oil in a large frying pan and fry the meatballs in 2 batches for 5 mins each until golden, then remove and set aside. Add the tomatoes to the pan and fry for 2 mins, add the grains, remaining walnuts and spinach and stir until just the spinach has just wilted. Return the meatballs to the pan, cover and heat through for 2-3 mins.
3. Meanwhile, mix the yoghurt and mustard together and serve with the stir fry.

CALIFORNIA WALNUT

16 SUNDAY

17 MONDAY

18 TUESDAY

19 WEDNESDAY

20 THURSDAY

21 FRIDAY

22 SATURDAY

CLEVER CLEANING TIPS

Freshen up your exercise trainers and bag

After a workout, sprinkle some baking soda inside your running shoes and gym bag to deodorise them. Leave the soda to work its magic, then simply tap it out before you use them again.

WISE WORDS

'Life shrinks or expands in proportion to one's courage.'

Anaïs Nin

REMEMBER THIS

Days out with Grandma

Shopping with grandparents was always a such a treat. They seemed to come alive in a shopping environment in a way that they never did at home. They seemed to know the price of absolutely everything. They also seemed to know everyone they met, and would always proudly show us off to all their friends. But most of all, they always made us feel really special.

Recipe of the week

APPLE AND BLACKBERRY CRUMBLE BARS

SERVES: **8** PREP TIME: **15 mins** COOK TIME: **35-40 mins**

1 Bramley cooking apple, peeled, cored and cut into small cubes (approx 100g)
150g (5oz) frozen blackberries
200g (7oz) light brown sugar plus 1 tbsp for filling
250g (9oz) wholemeal flour plus 1 tbsp for filling
100g (3.5oz) oats
1 egg
½ tsp mixed spice (optional)
125g (4oz) unsalted butter, melted

1. Preheat the oven to 200°C/180°C Fan/Gas Mark 6.
2. In a small mixing bowl, combine the cubed apple and frozen blackberries with 1 tbsp light brown sugar and 1 tbsp flour. Set to one side.
3. In a larger mixing bowl, combine the oats, light brown sugar, flour and mixed spice (if using) with a spoon. Mix in the egg and melted butter with the spoon, then get your hands in the bowl and bring the mixture together until it forms clusters.
4. Pour two-thirds of the crumbly mixture into a square tin and lightly press down with your fingers to create an even layer. Spread the apple and blackberry mixture on top, then sprinkle the remaining third of the crumble mix over the top. Don't worry if there are gaps, you want to see the fruit coming through.
5. Place in the oven and bake for 35-40 mins until golden on top and the apple is cooked through. Leave to cool before portioning into 8 bars and serving.

UK FLOUR MILLERS

23	SUNDAY

24	MONDAY

25	TUESDAY

26	WEDNESDAY

27	THURSDAY

28	FRIDAY

29	SATURDAY

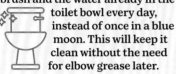
CLEVER CLEANING TIPS

A little daily clean goes a long way

Swish your toilet with your cleaning brush and the water already in the toilet bowl every day, instead of once in a blue moon. This will keep it clean without the need for elbow grease later.

WISE WORDS

'The two most important days in your life are the day you are born and the day you find out why.' Mark Twain

REMEMBER THIS

Perfect pasta

No meal we ever had was quite as satisfying as Auntie Rosa's extra-special spaghetti bolognaise. In those days, there were far fewer opportunities to enjoy such things as there are today. But it wasn't just the novelty of the dish that made this particular meal so memorable. It was the richness of the sauce and the beautifully judged succulence of the meat. Perfection.

Recipe of the week

CARBONARA-STYLE CAESAR AND MUSHROOM SPAGHETTI

SERVES: **4** PREP TIME: **10 mins** COOK TIME: **10-15 mins**

350g (12oz) spaghetti
1 tbsp olive oil
300g (10oz) pack smoked back bacon, diced
300g (10oz) mushrooms, sliced
1 medium egg, beaten
5 tbsp Cardini's Original Caesar Dressing
50g (2oz) Parmigiano Reggiano, finely grated, plus extra to serve

1. Cook the spaghetti according to the pack instructions.
2. Meanwhile, heat the oil in a large frying pan and fry the bacon for 4-5 mins until golden, then add the mushrooms and fry for a further 2-3 mins.
3. Mix the egg and Caesar Dressing in a bowl, then stir in the grated Parmesan.
4. Drain the spaghetti and add it to the bacon mixture. Stir in the egg mixture, then stir everything together over a low heat for 1-2 mins until evenly coated, adding a little splash of the pasta cooking water if needed.
5. Serve with extra shavings of Parmesan.

CARDINI'S

30	SUNDAY	*St Andrew's Day & First Sunday in Advent*

1	MONDAY	*St Andrew's Day (Bank Holiday Scotland)*

2	TUESDAY

3	WEDNESDAY

4	THURSDAY

5	FRIDAY

6	SATURDAY

CLEVER CLEANING TIPS

Use mouthwash to freshen up your washing machine

Eliminate musty smells in the washing machine by running an empty cycle with some mouthwash. This will keep your future washes smelling fresh.

WISE WORDS

'To tell a woman everything she cannot do is to tell her what she can.'

Spanish proverb

REMEMBER THIS?

A new 'do'

The Beehive, the Artichoke, the Bouffant, the Flick Up, the Pixie. We had them all at one point. Long and short. Blonde and brunette. We used to change our hairstyles more often than some men changed their socks. A new look always made us feel energised. We would almost feel reborn, as if we were a totally new woman. It was a lovely feeling... but it never lasted long.

Recipe of the week

CAMEMBERT & CARAMELISED ONION BREAD AND BUTTER PUDDING

SERVES: **4** PREP TIME: **5 mins** COOK TIME: **1 hour**

50g (2oz) Trewithen Dairy salted butter
3 red onions, thinly sliced
2 tbsp red wine vinegar
2 garlic cloves, peeled and grated
Small bunch of parsley, roughly chopped
100g (3.5oz) salted butter, softened, plus extra for greasing
1 loaf of bread (stale is fine), sliced
1 Camembert – or any mix of cheeses that need using up
200ml (7fl oz) Trewithen Dairy whole milk
2 eggs
50g (2oz) Trewithen Dairy Cornish clotted cream
1 tsp mustard

1. Heat the butter and a glug of olive oil over a medium heat, then add the onions and coat in the buttery oil. Cook for at least 20 mins, prodding from time to time, until they are all caramelised. Add the red wine vinegar and cook for a couple more minutes until sticky. Season with salt and pepper and set aside.
2. Stir the garlic, parsley and some black pepper into the softened butter, until thoroughly combined.
3. Spread the garlic butter over the bread on both sides. Slice the bread (including the crusts) into triangles.
4. Slice the Camembert into thick, oozy slices, if using. Otherwise, grate your own cheese.
5. Grease a baking dish and arrange a layer of bread in the bottom. Spoon over a layer of caramelised onions and cheese. Repeat with bread, onions and cheese until it's all used up.
6. Whisk the milk, eggs, clotted cream and mustard in a bowl, then season with salt and pepper. Pour over the bread until it is all soaked up. If you have the time, allow to stand for a little while so the bread really soaks up the mixture.
7. Preheat the oven to 180°C/160°C Fan/Gas Mark 4. Bake the pudding for 25 mins until bubbling and golden on top.

TREWITHEN DAIRY

7	SUNDAY

8	MONDAY

9	TUESDAY

10	WEDNESDAY

11	THURSDAY

12	FRIDAY

13	SATURDAY

CLEVER CLEANING TIPS

Keep your whites white

Using a sponge, add white vinegar to any sweat stains, then wash on a hot cycle, adding a gentle fabric-safe bleach for especially stubborn marks.

WISE WORDS

'One kind word can warm three winter months.'

Japanese proverb

REMEMBER THIS

Nativity plays

There was always a buzz of excitement. The sound of wooden blocks, glockenspiels and triangles providing the music. The simple costumes: rubber bands and tea towels providing the shepherds' headdresses. The teachers sternly reprimanding anyone who waved to their parents in the audience. The children shouting their lines. The flashing of cameras. Another school nativity play.

Recipe of the week

BAKED LEEK, STILTON AND WALNUT RISOTTO

SERVES: **4** PREP TIME: **5 mins** COOK TIME: **30 mins**

2 leeks, cut into thick pieces
300g (10.5oz) arborio rice
900ml (32 fl oz) vegetable stock
150g (5oz) soft, Philadelphia-style cheese
120g (4oz) Stilton, roughly crumbled
A small handful of walnut halves, roughly crushed

1. Heat the oven to 200°C/180°C Fan/Gas Mark 6.
2. Heat a drizzle of oil in a non-stick frying pan, or a pan that works on the hob and in the oven with a lid.
3. Add the leeks and fry on a medium heat for 5 mins, using the back of a spoon to push out the separate leek layers.
4. Add the arborio rice and stir on the heat for 1 min. Add the stock, season with salt and pepper and bring to a steady boil. If you've used a frying pan, tip the risotto into an ovenproof dish with a lid.
5. Cook in the oven for 20-25 mins until the rice is cooked, stirring once, halfway through.
6. Remove from the oven and stir in the soft cheese and most of the crumbled Stilton, reserving some for the topping.
7. Sprinkle with the crushed walnuts, the reserved Stilton and some ground black pepper. Serve with rocket leaves.

BRITISH LEEKS

14	SUNDAY

15	MONDAY

16	TUESDAY

17	WEDNESDAY

18	THURSDAY

19	FRIDAY

20	SATURDAY

CLEVER CLEANING TIPS

Use windshield repellent to keep your shower dry

Spray on the water repellent coating and wipe off any excess to prevent those annoying hard water stains.

WISE WORDS

'Nothing ever seems too bad, too hard, or too sad when you've got a Christmas tree in the living room.'

Nora Roberts

REMEMBER THIS

Decorating the tree

It was a vital part of the pre-Christmas ritual: selecting exactly the right ornaments to go on the Christmas tree. We would always make a concerted effort to include our own creations, lovingly made during art lessons at school. These were often fragile enough to collapse as we put them on. The real battle would come over who would be chosen for the honour of placing the angel on top.

Recipe of the week

CHRISTMAS TREE HONEY AND SPICE COOKIES

SERVES: **4** PREP TIME: **20 mins** COOK TIME: **10 mins**

3 tbsp Rowse Runny Honey
150g (5oz) butter
250g (9oz) plain flour
1 tbsp baking powder
1 tsp ground ginger
1 tsp cinnamon
50g (2oz) icing sugar
Edible decorations of your choice

1. Gently heat the honey and butter together, then leave to cool slightly.
2. In a bowl, mix the flour, baking powder, ginger and cinnamon. Add the honey and butter. Roll the dough out on a flour-dusted surface and cut out cookies with a cookie cutter.
3. Bake for around 10 mins at 180°C/160°C Fan/Gas Mark 4 watching until the cookies start to go slightly golden. Then leave to cool.
4. Mixing icing sugar with water to form a paste and drizzle over cookies. Add your decorations.

ROWSE HONEY

21	SUNDAY	*Winter Solstice (Shortest day)*

22	MONDAY

23	TUESDAY

24	WEDNESDAY

25	THURSDAY	*Christmas Day (Bank Holiday)*

26	FRIDAY	*Boxing Day (Bank Holiday)*

27	SATURDAY

CLEVER CLEANING TIPS

Use duct tape to collect pine needles

To collect every last pine needle when taking down your Christmas tree, loop a piece of cellotape or duct tape around your hand, sticky-side out, then pat the area where your tree was standing.

WISE WORDS

'Mankind is a great, an immense family. This is proved by what we feel in our hearts at Christmas.'
Pope John XXIII

REMEMBER THIS

The perfect present

It seemed too much to hope for. Could this really, finally be it? The one thing we'd been hinting at since summer began? It certainly seemed about the right shape and size. Pulling the last scraps of wrapping paper away, the final truth was revealed. This was it! The dream bike! At last! Now all we would have to do was learn how to ride it!

Recipe of the week

BAILEYS PROFITEROLE STACK

MAKES: **36 profiteroles** PREP TIME: **30 mins**
COOK TIME: **30 mins**

100g (3.5oz) butter, cut into 1cm cubes
140g (5oz) plain flour
4 eggs
600ml (21 fl oz) double cream
200ml (7 fl oz) Baileys, split into two equal batches
200g (7oz) dark chocolate, broken into pieces

1. Preheat oven to 200°C/180°C Fan/Gas Mark 6. Put the butter and 250ml (9 fl oz) water into a saucepan and heat over a medium heat until butter comes to a boil.
2. Turn off the heat and add in the flour, beating with a wooden spoon until a soft dough is formed.
3. Turn the heat back up to medium and cook out the flour for 3-4 mins, stirring constantly. Transfer to a large mixing bowl and leave to cool slightly.
4. Using an electric hand whisk, add the eggs one by one, ensuring you thoroughly incorporate each one until a smooth glossy paste is formed. Transfer into a piping bag and cut off the end to create a 1.5cm opening.
5. Pipe 18 small mounds onto each of two baking trays, then bake for 20 mins until risen and golden-brown. Leave the profiteroles to cool completely.
6. Pour the double cream and 100ml of Baileys into a mixing bowl and whisk until thick. Cut each profiterole in half and fill with cream, being careful not to overfill.
7. Heat the other 100ml of Baileys in a saucepan until just simmering, then remove from the heat and add the dark chocolate, stirring continuously until you have a smooth and glossy ganache.
8. Stack the profiteroles in a pyramid on a serving plate, spooning the ganache over each layer to help them stick. Drizzle with the remaining ganache and serve.

EASY PEASY BAKING CAMPAIGN, LAUNCHED BY UK FLOUR MILLERS

28	SUNDAY	

29	MONDAY	

30	TUESDAY	

31	WEDNESDAY	*New Year's Eve/Hogmanay*

1	THURSDAY	*New Year's Day (Bank Holiday)*

2	FRIDAY	*Bank Holiday (Scotland)*

3	SATURDAY	

Bag it

CLEVER CLEANING TIPS

Gather up your little kitchen items, from water bottle tops and lids to small food storage containers etc, and put them in a mesh laundry bag. Put this in your dishwasher next time you're turning it on and let it work its magic – they'll emerge clean as a whistle ready for you to use again.

WISE WORDS

'The greatest glory in living lies not in never failing, but in rising every time we fail.'
Nelson Mandela

REMEMBER THIS?

Festive feasts

When family came over at Christmas time it was always the same. Mum would get into a panic. Were there enough potatoes for everyone? Was the gravy too lumpy? Was the turkey cooked? Dad carved the turkey and portioned out the stuffing and sausage meat so everyone got their fair share. Granny, meanwhile, had already had one sherry too many and was laughing a bit too much as she attempted to read out her own joke from the cracker. And sometimes we'd even be allowed the smallest sip of Babycham.

Recipe of the week

CHRISTMAS LEFTOVER VEGETABLE KORMA

SERVES: **4** PREP TIME: **10 mins** COOK TIME: **30 mins**

1 tbsp olive oil
1 onion, finely chopped
3 garlic cloves, finely chopped
5cm piece ginger, peeled and finely sliced
1 red chilli, deseeded and finely chopped
2 tsp garam masala
1 tsp ground turmeric
100g (3.5oz) ground almonds
400g (14oz) tin chopped tomatoes
1 vegetable stock cube, made up to 400ml (14 fl oz)
200g (7oz) long-grain rice
500g (18oz) leftover roasted vegetables, such as potatoes, carrots, parsnips or butternut squash
200ml (7fl oz) double cream
Handful fresh coriander, to garnish

1. Heat the oil in a large saucepan or casserole dish over a medium-low heat. Add the onion and cook for 10 mins until softened. Stir in the garlic, ginger and chilli and cook for 1 min until fragrant. Stir in the garam masala, turmeric and ground almonds.
2. Pour in the chopped tomatoes and stock. Stir well, then simmer for 15 mins until thickened.
3. Wash the rice well in a sieve, then tip into a saucepan. Add 400ml (14 fl oz) water and a pinch of salt. Bring to a simmer, then cover and cook for 12 mins until tender.
4. Add the roasted vegetables and double cream to the curry, stir to combine and cook for 5 mins until heated through. Serve with the rice.

TESCO REAL FOOD

2025
year-to-view calendar

JANUARY

M		6	13	20	27	
Tu		7	14	21	28	
W	1	8	15	22	29	
Th	2	9	16	23	30	
F	3	10	17	24	31	
Sa	4	11	18	25		
Su	5	12	19	26		

FEBRUARY

M		3	10	17	24	
Tu		4	11	18	25	
W		5	12	19	26	
Th		6	13	20	27	
F		7	14	21	28	
Sa	1	8	15	22		
Su	2	9	16	23		

MARCH

M		3	10	17	24	31
Tu		4	11	18	25	
W		5	12	19	26	
Th		6	13	20	27	
F		7	14	21	28	
Sa	1	8	15	22	29	
Su	2	9	16	23	30	

APRIL

M		7	14	21	28	
Tu	1	8	15	22	29	
W	2	9	16	23	30	
Th	3	10	17	24		
F	4	11	18	25		
Sa	5	12	19	26		
Su	6	13	20	27		

MAY

M		5	12	19	26	
Tu		6	13	20	27	
W		7	14	21	28	
Th	1	8	15	22	29	
F	2	9	16	23	30	
Sa	3	10	17	24	31	
Su	4	11	18	25		

JUNE

M		2	9	16	23	30
Tu		3	10	17	24	
W		4	11	18	25	
Th		5	12	19	26	
F		6	13	20	27	
Sa		7	14	21	28	
Su	1	8	15	22	29	

JULY

M		7	14	21	28	
Tu	1	8	15	22	29	
W	2	9	16	23	30	
Th	3	10	17	24	31	
F	4	11	18	25		
Sa	5	12	19	26		
Su	6	13	20	27		

AUGUST

M		4	11	18	25	
Tu		5	12	19	26	
W		6	13	20	27	
Th		7	14	21	28	
F	1	8	15	22	29	
Sa	2	9	16	23	30	
Su	3	10	17	24	31	

SEPTEMBER

M	1	8	15	22	29	
Tu	2	9	16	23	30	
W	3	10	17	24		
Th	4	11	18	25		
F	5	12	19	26		
Sa	6	13	20	27		
Su	7	14	21	28		

OCTOBER

M		6	13	20	27	
Tu		7	14	21	28	
W	1	8	15	22	29	
Th	2	9	16	23	30	
F	3	10	17	24	31	
Sa	4	11	18	25		
Su	5	12	19	26		

NOVEMBER

M		3	10	17	24	
Tu		4	11	18	25	
W		5	12	19	26	
Th		6	13	20	27	
F		7	14	21	28	
Sa	1	8	15	22	29	
Su	2	9	16	23	30	

DECEMBER

M	1	8	15	22	29	
Tu	2	9	16	23	30	
W	3	10	17	24	31	
Th	4	11	18	25		
F	5	12	19	26		
Sa	6	13	20	27		
Su	7	14	21	28		

Relax & Unwind

Big hair, big dress, big smile!

Douglas McPherson remembers the effervescent Alma Cogan, the chart-topping singing sensation of the Fifties who came to fame with hits including Dreamboat and Never Do the Tango With an Eskimo

Alma Cogan was a new star for a new era. In the pre-rock 'n' roll world of the Fifties, as Britain slowly recovered from the pounding of the Second World War, and televisions began appearing in living rooms, Cogan was one of the first singers to build her success on the small screen.

With her big dresses and huge smile, she exuded optimism. Both glamorous and friendly, and as happy to do a comedy skit with Benny Hill as she was to sing her hits, she was a star who appealed to all the family.

The country loved her, making her the highest-paid

British female entertainer of her time, the first to top the singles chart, and the first to have her own TV series.

Born in Whitechapel, East London on May 19, 1932, Cogan was named after silent film star Alma Taylor.

Her mother encouraged her into showbusiness and she won £5 in the Sussex Queen of Song contest when she was just 11.

By her mid-teens, Cogan was singing at tea dances and appearing in variety shows. At 18, she worked with the then unknown Audrey Hepburn in the chorus of High Button Shoes in the West End.

Universal appeal

Cogan's first single was the velvety and solemn ballad To Be Worthy of You, in 1952. But it was with the whimsical If I Had a Golden Umbrella, the following year, that she unveiled the sunny, upbeat delivery that would become her trademark. Producer Walter Ridley titled her 1955 EP The Girl With a Laugh in Her Voice, although the more alliterative nickname the Girl with the Giggle in Her Voice has caught on over the years.

Her first chart entry came later that year with her ode to a sailor, Bell Bottom Blues, which made No.4.

In 1955, she topped the chart – the first British female singer to do so – with the swinging Dreamboat.

In an age when radio was king, Cogan's fame spread through regular appearances singing on the comedy programmes Gently Bentley and Take it From Here. But as television took off, she was one of the first singers to exploit the medium. She appeared as a guest on many shows and headlined six episodes of The Alma Cogan Show in 1957.

Like many British singers of the time, Cogan predominantly covered American hits, including Why do Fools Fall in Love (Frankie Lymon and The Teenagers) and Sugartime (The McGuire Sisters). Some became hits for her, some not, but all were made her own by Cogan's sparkling delivery.

Her 1963 cut of Tell Him, originally waxed by The Exciters, missed the UK chart but hit No.10 in Sweden and sparked that nation's love affair with her.

Cogan managed her own career and was an astute businesswoman, but she made no enemies.

"She was universally loved," said her close friend, Lionel Blair. "The parties at Alma's flat were notorious. Cary Grant, Noël Coward, The Beatles, Sammy Davis Jr... they were all there."

Her lack of husband or boyfriends fuelled rumours about her love life

---

Despite her outgoing nature, Cogan protected her private life. Her lack of husband or boyfriends fuelled rumours about her love life.

She was said to have turned down a proposal from Cary Grant, and her sister claimed that she had an affair with John Lennon although it has never been confirmed.

The truth, perhaps, is that her only love was her career, to which she devoted all her energy.

Burning bright

The rise of The Beatles effectively ended Cogan's run as a British chart star.

Alma embraced the Fab Four's music. She recorded a glorious big band swing version of Eight Days a Week – and half a dozen other Beatles songs –

but in the public's eyes she epitomised the Fifties, and Sixties pop fans had no time for nostalgia.

Undaunted, Cogan pursued a career abroad, where fashion wasn't so fickle. At a concert in Japan, 38,000 people turned out to see her.

She recorded her songs in six languages and twice topped the Swedish hit parade, with Tennessee Waltz in 1964 and The Birds and the Bees in 1965.

Trying to recapture the zeitgeist in the UK and US, she recorded the novelty Love Ya Illya, a tribute to The Man From U.N.C.L.E. character played by David McCallum. Released in 1966 under the name Angela and The Fans, it didn't chart.

That same year, Cogan began treatment for cancer. Two months after her final TV appearance on International Cabaret, she died on October 26, aged 34.

Among the celebrities who attended her funeral was Carry On actor Jack Douglas, who said, "I don't think I have ever stood at a graveside and seen so many men crying their eyes out."

● The Alma Cogan International Fanclub is committed to honouring the memory of their favourite star. To find out more visit almacogan2018.com or email almacogan@gmail.com

QUICK CROSSWORD 1

ACROSS
1 Parliament clock tower (3, 3)
4 West End musical starring Lucie Jones (8)
10 Stradivarius user (9)
11 Severe (5)
12 Code word preceding Sierra (5)
13 Scintillation – of stars, eg (9)
14 - - - García Márquez, One Hundred Years of Solitude author (7)
16 Choux pastry confection (6)
19 80s coiffure (6)
21 Modern language group (7)
23 Oran or Constantine natives (9)
25 Lariat (5)
27 - - - Watts, Mulholland Drive star (5)
28 The Gentlemen actor (4, 5)
29 Inn (8)
30 Steamship worker (6)

DOWN
1 Refreshment (8)
2 Rub down – a horse, eg (5)
3 Leader in a newspaper (9)
5 Fred - - -, influential dancer (7)
6 Circuit (5)
7 Great academic knowledge (9)
8 Sledge (6)
9 Walther PPK, eg (6)
15 Louise - - -, French sculptor of large spiders (9)
17 Artificial illumination (9)
18 Newscaster (8)
20 Don (7)
21 Stand down (6)
22 Disembowel (6)
24 Cologne's river (5)
26 - - - up, move in together (5)

Puzzles

MUSIC QUIZ

1   What was Freddie Mercury's real name?

2   Which member of the Avengers had a brief stint as a pop star?

3   Which artist's entire 1985 Live Aid set consisted of just a single cover song?

4   What rock icon was the founder of The Society for the Prevention of Cruelty to Long-haired Men?

5   Before Phil Collins, who was the lead singer of Genesis?

6   Paul McCartney credits which artist with teaching him everything he knows?

7   Who was the first woman ever inducted into the Rock and Roll Hall of Fame?

8   Art Garfunkel initially declined to sing one of Simon & Garfunkel's biggest hits solo. Which song is it?

9   What other legendary vocalist is a cousin of Whitney Houston?

10   Which, now deceased, Eighties and Nineties pop singer was born Georgios Kyriacos Panayiotou?

11   What was the first music video to ever air on MTV?

12   U2 wrote the song 'Stuck in a Moment' about which late frontman?

13   What legendary pop group got their name from 'Brothers Gibb'?

14   Though it was made famous by Ike and Tina Turner, Proud Mary was first recorded by whom?

15   Cher's first single referenced which rock star?

Were you right?
Turn to page 182 for the answers

Teed Off

Why did Anna always have to be so competitive?

Short story

I gazed up at the clear blue sky and sighed. What I wanted more than anything was to get off the course. When I go on holiday, all I want to do is relax, read a book or two, laze on the beach. As a postman, I get more than enough exercise at work. The last thing on my list was any kind of sport.

Our neighbours are keen golfers so we sometimes play a round of golf with them. I don't mind, it's a pleasant enough way to spend an afternoon, but for me it's just a game, and games are meant to be fun.

Unfortunately, my wife is not like that. It doesn't matter what we play – cards, Pictionary, Scrabble, she's only happy when she wins.

Anna's voice snapped me from my daydream.

"Your turn. You're already two shots behind on this hole."

More by luck than judgment, my last shot wasn't bad. Even with my lack of skill I should be able to sink the ball, but as I got ready to play my shot, my wife tutted. Loudly.

"You need to stand a bit more to the right. Like this." Before I could object, she'd grabbed hold of my arm and moved me into position. "That's better."

I muttered something rude under my breath. That was another thing about my wife that drove me crazy. If there was a chance she might actually lose, Anna resorted to all kinds of shady tactics to put me off my game.

"What did you say?" she asked.

"Oh nothing, darling. Nothing at all," I replied through tightly clenched teeth. "Maybe you should just let me try a few shots on my own."

That way I might actually win a hole, I thought, but I didn't say that.

She shrugged. "Of course, it's up to you but you'll never improve if you're not willing to learn." She paused meaningfully. "I AM winning you know. And don't forget, there's lunch at stake."

Even before I struck the ball, I could feel her eyes boring into the back of my neck. As she hoped, it was enough to put me off.

I watched in dismay as the ball wobbled off to the left, coming to rest a couple of inches short of the hole.

It doesn't matter what we play, she's only happy when she wins

---

"Oh, bad luck," said Anna as she tapped her ball home. "That's another win for me."

She picked up her ball and strode over to the next hole. "Hurry up, Stephen. Let's not keep people waiting."

By then, I'd had enough. All I could think about was heading to the beach and getting something to eat, even if I did have to pay for it.

"As you've won every hole so far, can't we just stop here? There's no way I can catch you up."

She stared at me as if I was insane.

"Don't be daft, Stephen. The last hole is the best one." She paused. "How about I let you go first for a change? Will that do?"

I nodded. I'd already lost the match, the least I could do was to try to win the last hole. As I got ready to take my shot, I expected Anna to intervene but she stayed where she was.

Without the benefit of my wife's 'help', the ball went exactly where I wanted it to go, managing to avoid all the obstacles. When it slowed down and stopped, it wasn't very far from the hole. With a bit of luck, I should be able to get the ball in with my next shot.

I stepped away, unable to keep the grin from my face.

"Not bad," said Anna with grudging admiration.

"Thanks."

She'd need to be very lucky or very accurate to win this one but that didn't stop her trying.

It tickled me to see how much trouble she went to, trying to win that final hole – kneeling down, closing one eye, measuring the angle, changing position several times. Thank goodness it was the last one. I couldn't wait to get off the course.

After what felt like ages, Anna finally hit the ball. It started off well, but just when I thought she might land a hole in one, the ball veered off to the right, bounced, and was away.

I holed my ball with my next shot, then stood back to watch as Anna tried to recover from her hopeless position. It took three more shots before she managed to finish the round.

"I think you'll find I've won that one," I said.

I put an enormous tick on my side of the score card and handed it to her. She'd beaten me by 17 holes to one, which was pretty bad, even for me, but at least I'd avoided a whitewash.

Anna stood there, staring at the card. She looked so disappointed, I hugged her.

"Don't worry, darling. You can't expect to win every hole, not even when we're playing crazy golf."

I gave her a peck on the cheek.

"Right. Let's go and get something to eat. The fish and chips are on me."

BY LINDA LEWIS. PIC: SHUTTERSTOCK CREATIVE

The Jersey boys done good

Frankie Valli & The Four Seasons conquered the pop world. Simon Button takes a look at the band that survived and thrived before and after the British invasion

Behind the music

When The Four Seasons stormed to the top of the US charts with Sherry in 1962, they were an overnight sensation – albeit one that was nine years in the making. Fronted by Frankie Valli, the New Jersey foursome had gone through many names and several line-up changes, suffering a string of flops before the catchy doo-wop song finally put them on the map.

Born Francesco Castelluccio, Valli was the son of an Italian barber and a high-school dropout who cut hair and worked in construction while dreaming of a singing career. He was still a teenager when, in the early Fifties, guitarist Tommy DeVito heard his distinctive falsetto and invited him to sing with his band the Variety Trio.

He and DeVito formed The Variatones and eventually The Four Lovers, releasing The Apple of My Eye to minor success, followed by half a dozen that failed to chart. But they kept at it, going through nearly 20 band names and a few shifts in personnel before settling on The Four Seasons with Valli on vocals, DeVito on guitar, Nick Massi on bass and Bob Gaudio on keyboards.

Sherry baby
Gaudio turned out to be a genius choice. The Four Seasons looked like they were set for a career as session musicians for producer Bob Crewe, until Gaudio, who was 15 when he wrote the novelty hit Short Shorts for The Royal Teens, came up with Sherry in just 15 minutes.

Frankie liked the song, the other guys didn't, but Crewe had the casting vote and it changed the band's fortunes forever. Luckily, Gaudio had at least two more aces up his sleeve: Big Girls Don't Cry (inspired by a line from a John Payne Western called Tennessee's Partner) and

Walk Like a Man. Legend has it that, while they were recording the latter, the room above the studio caught fire, but producer Crewe was so determined to complete the session he blocked the door and firemen had to break it down with an axe. Crewe's foolhardiness paid off. The song became the band's third US chart-topper in a row.

Frankie's falsetto was a big draw for record buyers, although he later noted: "Falsetto wasn't something new. The R&B groups had been using it for years, but as background. We began to use it doing the lead singing in a high falsetto. That's what created the signature sound." It served them well. During the Sixties they went on to sell an incredible 80 million records, with other notable hits including Stay, Let's Hang On and Working My Way Back to You.

The group had connections with the Mob, albeit tenuous ones

Beneath the veneer
While they were presented as clean-cut young men who sang about falling in love and other issues faced by ordinary working-class folk, all was not as it seemed. As revealed in the musical about their lives, Jersey Boys, they had something of a chequered past.

DeVito did jail time for petty crimes. They also had connections with the Mob, albeit tenuous ones. Captain of New York's Genovese crime family Angelo 'Gyp' DeCarlo was often in the bars where the Four Seasons performed in the early days. Gaudio recalled that at one point "We were being leaned on by a Mob faction from Brooklyn, claiming they owned us for no real good reason except that they had a connection with a manager we had early on" and DeCarlo helped sort it out.

Bassist Nick Massi lasted until 1965, while Tommy DeVito quit in 1970 because he was tired of life on the road, just as the group's business empire had begun to unravel. Debts were piling up, with Valli recalling: "We were having some internal problems, we had to buy our partners out and so forth. It got very confusing." The debts totalled $1.4 million, which Frankie and Bob Gaudio took it upon themselves to repay. When their deal with Motown in 1972 turned sour, Valli spent his own money for the rights to My Eyes Adored You and enjoyed a solo hit in the process.

The million-seller began another sensational chart run, with Frankie foregoing the falsetto and the band adopting the new disco sound for such smashes as Who Loves You, Silver Star and the UK-only release The Night. One of The Four Seasons' last hits was 1975's December 1963 (Oh, What a Night), although their legacy endures thanks to their induction into the Rock and Roll Hall of Fame and the success of the Jersey Boys show.

Valli continued to tour with various incarnations of the band, saying: "Nobody can put you down for trying," he added. "That's what life is all about and if you think you might be good for something you should try it. So you fall on your face? You get right back up."

Strangers on a Train

Could Ewan really be as exciting as Jill imagined?

Short story

Most days, Jill Masters drove to work. But on Fridays, she took the train, as she found it a lot less stressful than battling the Friday rush-hour traffic.

On some of the commutes, she would read. Other times she'd tackle a crossword.

But that Friday evening, she decided to indulge in a game she had recently devised that involved her fellow passengers.

Jill decided to impress him by acting cool, calm and collected

---

After carefully studying each of them for a few moments, Jill would invent little tales about who they might be and the thrilling lives they might lead.

As she cast her eyes around the carriage, Jill found herself smiling when she spotted Ewan.

He was one of the regular commuters, with whom she'd struck up a friendly conversation one evening when the train they were on had been delayed.

Jill had been hoping to catch Ewan's eye when she boarded the train that evening, only he had his head stuck in a notepad.

Although she was curious as to what he might be doing, the angle of the seats made it impossible for her to see the pad properly.

Moving on from Ewan, Jill turned her attention to the young woman next to him.

With her long blonde hair and icy-blue eyes, she was like an Austrian princess.

What if her name was Countess von Tesselhof and she was descended from German royalty? Perhaps her family had fled to England following the upheaval of the First World War.

Having allowed her imagination to run riot, Jill turned and glanced out of the window as the train pulled into a station.

It was far more likely that the young lady in question was a Sally or a Debbie, and worked in an office. Nevertheless, Jill preferred her version of the woman's life.

Jill waited until the train had pulled out of the station again before studying the fresh batch of passengers.

Her eyes were drawn to an elderly woman who wore her grey hair in a bun.

She looked innocent enough, but what if, in her youth, she had been one of the most promising young actresses of her generation, Verity Grainger.

Naturally, Hollywood had come calling, but Verity had turned them down. Preferring the quiet life, she had finally retired to a village in Devon, and helped out at the local wildlife sanctuary.

Having established Verity's true identity, Jill chuckled.

She was just about to turn her attention elsewhere, when she noticed that Ewan was watching her.

With a gasp of sudden realisation, something dawned on Jill.

What if Ewan worked for the Secret Service and his role was to recruit people who had the potential to become special agents?

Maybe he'd previously engaged Jill in conversation because he considered her to be an excellent candidate.

Bearing this in mind, as the train pulled into her station, Jill decided to impress him by acting cool, calm and collected.

Her plan worked impeccably – until she stumbled into Ewan as they disembarked.

"I'm sorry," she apologised.

The collision had caused Ewan to drop his notepad, so Jill bent down to retrieve it for him.

"No!" Ewan cried.

But it was too late.

As Jill retrieved the pad, she soon realised that it wasn't a notepad at all.

It was, in fact, a sketchpad.

Glancing through it, Jill discovered that Ewan had been drawing various passengers.

The last sketch was of her.

"No offence," Ewan said, embarrassed. "During the commute home, I like to sketch my fellow passengers and make up little stories about them."

"So, what tale have you concocted about me?" Jill asked, as she handed him back the drawings.

Sensing she wasn't going to allow him to escape without an explanation, Ewan confessed.

"I thought you might be an undercover spy, although I haven't made up my mind what case you're working on at present."

Jill laughed.

"I told you it was silly," he mumbled.

Jill decided it was time for her to confess too.

"Can I let you into a little secret?" she said.

"Please do."

"I play a very similar game."

Momentarily, Ewan was too surprised to reply. Then he started to laugh.

Finding the laughter infectious, Jill joined in.

She wasn't going to allow him to escape without an explanation

---

"I don't suppose you fancy grabbing a quick drink?" she asked, deciding to take a chance. "Maybe you could try to work out my true identity as we chat."

"Now that sounds like an excellent plan," Ewan replied.

As they wandered away in search of a suitable pub, Jill wondered how their tale might unfold.

BY TONY HAYNES. PIC: SHUTTERSTOCK CREATIVE

QUICK CROSSWORD 2

ACROSS

1 Like a white-tie occasion (6)
4 Broke the law (8)
9 2016 voter's option? (6)
10 Tangerine-like fruit (8)
12 Gang (4)
13 - - - road, unbaked confection (5)
14 Tesla or Ohm, eg (4)
17 Dogged (6-6)
20 - - - the motions, performing without sincerity (5, 7)
23 Cut roughly (4)
24 Bruised (5)
25 - - - Call Me Mister Tibbs!, Sidney Poitier sequel film (4)
28 Decompression sickness (3, 5)
29 Sober (6)
30 Fine (8)
31 Robinson - - -, Daniel Defoe novel (6)

DOWN

1 Citadel (8)
2 Cud-chewing animal (8)
3 Ardent (4)
5 Mary Shelley novel (12)
6 Nelson - - -, 1930s actor and baritone (4)
7 Bold (6)
8 Make a contribution (6)
11 Comedian and actor who starred in The Square Peg (6, 6)
15 Blossom (5)
16 Like Robin Hood's men? (5)
18 Hardhearted (8)
19 Indigenous people of the Great Plains (8)
21 Roofing material (6)
22 Conceal (6)
26 Brown - - -, British musket (4)
27 Square number (4)

Puzzles

SPORTS QUIZ

1 Before Andy Murray, who was the last British tennis player to win a men's singles Grand Slam tournament?

2 Which footballer has scored the most goals in World Cup history?

3 After retiring from professional cycling, in what other sport did Bradley Wiggins briefly attempt to make a career?

4 The Los Angeles Lakers and New York Knicks play which sport?

5 Which England footballer was famously never given a yellow card?

6 In American Football, how many points do you score for a touchdown?

7 How many balls are there in total on the table at the start of a game of snooker?

8 At which Olympics did Kelly Holmes win two gold medals?

9 Which sport involves tucks and pikes?

10 In which sport is 180 deemed a perfect score?

11 What was Muhammad Ali's real name?

12 Which country's rugby team is called The Springboks?

13 Modern pentathlon involves running, shooting and horse riding. Which other two sports are featured?

14 The Fosbury Flop is a technique used in which sport?

15 Which sports presenter is credited with devising Mo Farah's celebratory 'Mobot' dance?

Were you right?
Turn to page 182 for the answers

Flooded With Love

Surely nothing else could go wrong for Jenna?

Short story

As she opened the front door, Jenna heard the sound of running water, and cursed. She'd obviously left a tap on – talk about pregnancy brain.

Giving a frustrated sigh, she walked into the kitchen only to see a torrent of water gushing across the floor.

Her hand leapt to her mouth in horror and tears pricked her eyes.

What had gone wrong now? Honestly, it had been one thing after another lately.

A few weeks ago, one of the garden fences had blown down, and then only the other day her car had decided not to start. Nothing terrible in the grand scheme of things and all solvable, but because she was feeling extra sensitive, each problem had seemed like some enormous test of fate.

Squaring her shoulders, she grabbed some towels from the nearby laundry basket and flung them on top of the deluge, trying to stem the flow as best she could before she turned off the stopcock.

How she wished Mark were here. She took a shuddering breath, remembering times past when something would go wrong and her husband would make some witty retort to try and make her laugh. Or just hold her tight, telling her it would all be OK.

It wasn't as if she hadn't known what sort of life she'd lead being married to a man in the armed forces.

You had to learn to be self-sufficient or rely on family and friends and she was very grateful she had both close by. But it wasn't the same as having the man she loved there beside her.

Focusing on the emergency at hand, she reached for the list of numbers she kept handy and made a call. "Help! There's water all over the kitchen. Looks like it's a burst pipe and I'm pregnant."

She wasn't sure why she added that last bit.

It must be her hormones talking as they were all over the place.

"No problem. Have you turned the water off?"

"Yes."

"We'll get someone out to you as soon as we can."

With help on the way, Jenna gazed at the soggy mess surrounding her.

She'd just been for a check-up for her and the baby.

Everything was going well and she was due any day now. And, didn't things go in threes?

Her hand leapt to her mouth in horror and tears pricked her eyes

---

Surely that must mean from now on things would go well?

She was still mopping up when she heard the doorbell.

"Hi, I'm Moses from Joe's Plumbers. You said there was an emergency?"

Jenna stared at him in disbelief and saw him grin.

"Yeah, I know, parting of the water with my staff and all that. Except, I've got a spanner and mole grips instead."

Jenna chuckled. "It's an apt name for a plumber."

"That's why I got the job, they said. Well, that and a few years' experience."

Jenna explained what had happened and watched as Moses set to work.

"It shouldn't take too long to fix." He tilted his head, his gaze on her stomach. "So when's the baby due?"

Jenna rubbed her hands protectively over her bump.

"Any day now. Our first."

"Nice. Bet you and your husband can't wait."

Jenna nodded with feeling. She was fed up with waddling everywhere and not being able to find a comfortable position to sit.

"Mark is in the forces but he's hoping to be back in time for the birth."

She gazed at the wet towels soaking up the water and her shoulders slumped. The washing machine would be going flat out and struggling to bend over and pick up wet towels feeling like a beached whale was not her idea of fun.

Having settled up, Moses gave her an encouraging look.

"I'm sure he'll be back in time. He'll have it written in stone on his calendar, he will. Too much of an important day to miss, so don't you worry."

He gave her a big smile and a wink before he stepped outside, whistling as he walked down the drive.

***

Holding her baby in her arms a few weeks later, Jenna and Mark gazed in awe at their new tiny bundle.

"He's just perfect," Mark breathed.

"He is," Jenna replied as she gently stroked her son's cheek with one finger. "We need to decide on a name."

Catching sight of a rainbow shining like a beacon of hope outside the hospital window, Jenna smiled as floods of unconditional love swept through her for her new bundle of joy.

"Well, what about calling him Noah?" She'd already recounted the story of the deluge to Mark.

"Perfect. Hello, Noah," Mark murmured softly.

Gently stroking her baby son's head, Jenna knew that life was never going to be the same again, but that was good. Change was good.

And right now, right this minute, she couldn't imagine any lovelier new beginning.

BY CARRIE HEWLETT. PIC: SHUTTERSTOCK CREATIVE

A-Wop-Bop-A-Loo-Bop...

Flamboyant Little Richard defined the sound of rock 'n' roll and influenced a whole generation of musicians, says Sean Egan

L ittle Richard was the originator, emancipator and architect of rock 'n' roll. His own words (he's never exactly been renowned for hiding his light under a bushel), but many agree with his claim to be the founding father of the genre.

Richard Wayne Penniman was born in Macon, Georgia in 1932, one of 12 children. Richard learned to play piano in the local church, his precociousness earning him the diminutive

prefix, one which, unlike Stevie Wonder, he never felt inclined to dispense with. Although weaned on gospel, the style of music for which Richard was destined was not quite so reverential, as epitomised in 1955 by his breakthrough hit Tutti Frutti. It established his signatures of slangy lyrics, breakneck instrumentation, and hollered, whoop-punctuated singing. It was also groundbreaking: Bill Haley's Rock Around the Clock was a hit first, Elvis Presley's That's All Right (Mama) was

recorded before it, but Tutti Frutti is now widely recognised as the first chart entry to epitomise the grit, volume and abandon that defines rock 'n' roll. Richard's family were partial to Bing Crosby and Ella Fitzgerald but, as he later explained, "I knew there was something that could be louder than that, but I didn't know where to find it. And I found it was me."

A saucy success
It was the start of a string of iconic smashes that included

Behind the music

Rip It Up, Long Tall Sally, She's Got It, The Girl Can't Help It, Lucille, Jenny Jenny, Good Golly Miss Molly and Ooh My Soul, songs that often had a composing contribution by Richard. Others proceeded to take their cue from him. Presley's hip-wriggling was patently the embodiment of the outrageousness and earthiness suffusing Richard's music. He also covered Richard's songs, as did Buddy Holly, Carl Perkins and, in amusingly more sedate renditions, Pat Boone.

In Britain, we took Richard so unequivocally to our hearts that we were even prepared to propel his softer fare into the hit parade: the biggest of his 15 top 40 entries here was his peculiar cover choice of Twenties standard Baby Face. It's somewhat astonishing that Richard achieved success at all considering the lewdness of his lyrics. When he implored Jenny to "Spin it like a spinning top," he wasn't talking about toys, while when he told Miss Molly "You sure like to ball," it wasn't dancing to which he was referring. He seemed to get away with the single entendres because the powers-that-be assumed they were gibberish on the level of "Awopbobaloobop Alopbamboom", the whirlwind of nonsense with which he famously opened Tutti Frutti.

A troubled idol

Richard's image was as flamboyant as his records – a towering pompadour atop a face sporting an immaculate pencil moustache and a shocking suspicion of mascara (not for nothing was his nickname the Georgia Peach). He was sartorially immaculate, but in a manner that suggested he was taking the mickey out of the very idea of smartness, particularly his ballooning trouser legs. Everybody got a good view of this look because he insisted on standing up as he played piano,

one of the devices he used to drive audiences into a frenzy. This caterwauling campiness was immortalised in the 1956 movie Don't Knock the Rock.

When Elvis told Richard he was "the greatest" Richard didn't disagree. 'The Handsomest Man in Rock 'n' Roll' was another, self-chosen, moniker. In mid-20th century America,

---

When Elvis told Richard he was 'the greatest' Richard didn't disagree

---

a black man thus preening – let alone visibly exciting the daughters of white people was a disturbing proposition.

The parents may have been outraged, but the upcoming generation of rockers were scribbling down notes. Robert Zimmerman, the future Bob Dylan, stated in his high-school yearbook that his ambition was "To join Little Richard." The Beatles so idolised Richard that they led an EP with Long Tall Sally. Yet even as the kids destined to become Sixties superstars were studying his modus operandi, Richard was disavowing it.

Richard believed the naysayers who deemed rock the devil's music, but with the additional twist that he seemed to blame his bisexuality – about which he was tormented – on his rockin'. All these things combined in 1957 to motivate him to ditch rock and switch to gospel, with disastrous artistic and commercial consequences. His subsequent career was spent mining the nostalgia circuit and switching back and forth in his belief in the harmful potential of rock.

Richard's heyday may be more than 60 years ago, but it has left an imperishable legacy, and not just in musical styles. "When I was a boy, the white people would sit upstairs," he reflected, "and the blacks was downstairs. The white kids would jump over the balcony and come down to dance with the blacks. We started that merging all across the country."

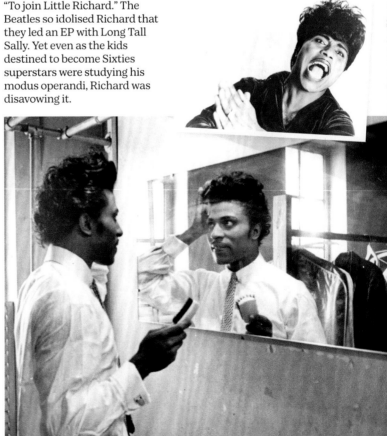

Beating the Clock

Penny's day was going from bad to worse

Short story

Penny glanced at her watch. She prided herself on being punctual. Unfortunately, she'd noticed the same courtesy wasn't always extended to her. For instance, the panel at the university where she was attending an interview that morning were running late.

Penny wouldn't have minded, only she'd offered to cover an afternoon shift at the

This may sound silly, but is your name Sandra by any chance?

fast-food restaurant where she worked.

She glanced at her watch again. She was just about to ring her supervisor and explain the situation when the head of the interview panel finally appeared.

"I'm sorry, only we're running a little late, I'm afraid," said the professor.

It's more than a little, Penny thought, but she didn't complain.

An hour and a half later, Penny's feelings were difficult to describe. On the one hand, she was extremely pleased with how she'd conducted herself during the interview. On the other, she'd tried to ring her shift supervisor to let him know she was running late, but couldn't get through.

As the bus she'd caught reached the outskirts of town, it became snarled up in heavy traffic. Penny sighed.

With her nerves on the point of fraying, she began to chew her fingernails. Biting her nails was always an indication she was stressed.

It wasn't just the interview that had been playing on her mind either. That evening, she was due to go on a blind date with a man named Kelvin,

arranged by her best friend, Jess. Never having been on a blind date before, Penny was feeling somewhat jittery.

All thoughts of the evening's date were far from her mind when the bus at last crept into the depot. When she finally arrived at the restaurant, Darren, her supervisor, was furious.

"I tried to ring several times," Penny explained, "but I couldn't get through."

"Trying isn't good enough," Darren grunted.

"But I'm never late."

"You mean you're never usually late."

"It won't happen again," Penny said. "I promise."

Darren begrudgingly accepted her apology, then said, "I'll need you to work an extra hour at the end of your shift to make up the time."

"Can I do an extra hour tomorrow instead, only…"

Darren's eyes narrowed. "Only what?"

"Nothing," she mumbled, defeated.

Try as she might, Penny simply couldn't make up the time she'd lost during the day, so she texted Kelvin to say she was running late.

She found it disconcerting that he didn't reply, but she forgave him the instant she arrived at the bar where they were due to meet, because he'd secured a lovely corner table overlooking the river.

"Hi," said Penny. "Kelvin? I'm sorry I'm late."

The man turned and looked at her with a quizzical expression.

Penny blushed.

"I beg your pardon," she stammered. "Are you Kelvin?"

"Erm, no," the bemused patron replied, smiling. He held out his hand and introduced himself. "I'm Alex."

As Penny shook his hand, she noted he had a lovely smile, though she dismissed the

thought when she retreated to the bar. It was a bit unfair to her blind date, after all.

She was just about to order a drink when her phone pinged. A text from Kelvin – short, curt and very much to the point.

"I waited for you for 20 minutes, but then I left. I hate people who are late."

After all she'd been through that day, Penny felt like crying. Life could be so unfair. She was just about to leave when Alex joined her at the bar.

Glancing at Penny, he bit his bottom lip, then said, "This may sound silly, but is your name Sandra by any chance?"

"I'm afraid not," said Penny.

"Oh, OK… sorry."

Alex blushed, then confessed, "Only, one of my work colleagues set me up on a blind date this evening and I've got the feeling I've been stood up."

Penny laughed.

"What's so funny?" Alex asked.

"I'm supposed to be on a blind date as well," Penny grinned. "Only, I've been stood up, too."

"At the risk of sounding incredibly cheeky, I don't suppose you'd allow me to buy you a drink?" Alex smiled, tentatively.

The man looked at her with a quizzical expression

It really was a lovely smile.

"Why not!" Penny said.

"So, what would you like?" Alex asked.

Penny considered carefully.

"Good conversation, a few laughs and a dash of mild flirting please."

"That sounds like a lovely cocktail, can I have one too?"

"Of course," Penny laughed.

As Alex ordered their drinks, Penny couldn't help wondering if being late wasn't so bad after all.

BY TONY HAYNES. PIC: SHUTTERSTOCK CREATIVE

QUICK CROSSWORD 3

ACROSS

1 University don (6)
5 - - - Love, John Denver and Plácido Domingo duet (7)
9 Male singers (9)
10 Seaweed used in popular Welsh dish (5)
11 All the more, yet (4)
12 Icy abode (5)
13 Creamy cheese (4)
16 Seabird (9)
18 Dormant (5)
19 Entertain (5)
21 Under the sea (9)
23 After that (4)
24 Auxiliary (5)
26 Pour (down) (4)
29 2005 romcom with Will Smith and Eva Mendes (5)
30 Inferior (5-4)
31 Robert - - -, TV scientist and life peer (7)
32 - - - Jackson, actress and former politician (6)

DOWN

2 Sincere (7)
3 Tardy (4)
4 Vessel for claret (9)
5 Basil-based sauce (5)
6 Character in a play (4)
7 Antagonistic, hostile (7)
8 Town-centre performance (6, 7)
9 Morning broadcast (9, 4)
14 Spun fibres of flax (5)
15 City in northern Italy (5)
17 Boarding (9)
20 (Of food) leftover (7)
22 Eire (7)
25 Vladimir - - -, president of Russia (5)
27 Lead pellets (4)
28 Eric - - -, Python (4)

FILM QUIZ

1 What are the dying words of Charles Foster Kane in Citizen Kane?

2 What TV show was Jack Nicholson referencing when he ad-libbed "Here's Johnny!" in The Shining?

3 The head of what kind of animal is front-and-centre in an infamous scene from The Godfather?

4 Who played park owner John Hammond in Jurassic Park?

5 In what 1976 thriller does Robert De Niro famously say "You talkin' to me?"

6 Marlon Brando "could have been a contender" in what iconic 1954 crime drama?

7 In what 1950 drama does Bette Davis say, "Fasten your seatbelts; it's going to be a bumpy night"?

8 In Risky Business, what song did Tom Cruise famously lip-sync to in his underwear?

9 Who is the only actor to receive an Oscar nomination for acting in a Lord of the Rings movie?

10 For which 1964 musical blockbuster did Julie Andrews win the Academy Award for Best Actress?

11 Which movie was incorrectly announced as the winner of Best Picture at the 2017 Academy Awards, during one of the biggest Oscars flubs?

12 Which 1948 Alfred Hitchcock movie starred James Stewart and was shot to look like one continuous take?

13 "Well, nobody's perfect" is the final line from what classic 1959 comedy starring Marilyn Monroe?

14 In what 1979 James Bond movie does the spy go to outer space?

15 What is the name of Quint's shark-hunting boat in Jaws?

Were you right?
Turn to page 182 for the answers

Hidden Hideaway

Karen's secret escape was anything but exclusive

"Did you have a good holiday in Menorca?" I asked my neighbour Dee. We'd bumped into each other at the corner shop.

She nodded.

"It was fabulous! Barrie and I stumbled across this gorgeous, secluded beach. It was practically deserted, so we had it all to ourselves."

"It sounds like heaven."

"It was like our own little secret escape, Karen. Soft, silky sand, crystal-clear sea, beautiful blue sky, plus peace and quiet. We spent every day there."

Dee showed me the pics. The sun-kissed cove was indeed lovely and, as she'd said, practically deserted. I didn't see a single sunbather or swimmer in the photos.

My husband Ian and I were planning a holiday, but we hadn't decided where to go. This looked perfect!

"There's a bit of a catch to this paradise, though," Dee went on, as the queue inched along. "There's a flight of narrow wooden steps that lead down to the beach – but I can guarantee it's worth the hike."

After I'd paid for my groceries, I headed home and told Ian all about it.

"So this secret escape isn't far from the actual resort they stayed at?" he asked.

"It's a short stroll further along. She gave me the name of their travel agent. We can book it online with Fly U Today. Why don't we take a look at their packages?" I suggested, as I put the shopping away.

"OK, but I have a funny sort of feeling there's something amiss about this secret escape," he said.

Ian was a natural cynic, so I wasn't surprised by his remark.

"What do you mean?"

"Well, can we trust their word, Karen? Dee and Barrie have always been a bit quirky and eccentric, haven't they? Do you remember when Dee dyed her hair bright pink, for no apparent reason? And then Barrie suddenly bought that rusty old caravan on impulse? It was stuck on their driveway for months until he finally sold it for scrap."

"But I saw the pics myself," I replied. "The beach was unbelievably quiet."

Ian found the Fly U Today website easily, but before he began, he turned to me.

"What if it's a nudist beach?" he whispered.

"Don't be silly!" I giggled.

Before long, we found the resort in Menorca, and booked a package to fly out in a month's time.

We decided to stay in a different hotel from Barrie and Dee, though.

On the day of travel, everything went smoothly.

The sun-kissed cove was indeed lovely

We checked into the hotel and unpacked.

"There's no rush to find this secret escape," Ian said. "Let's just chill out for a few days first."

I nodded. I was looking forward to sunbathing, swimming in the hotel pool and sampling the jacuzzi!

On day three, we packed a bag for the beach and set out to find Dee and Barrie's recommendation.

We ambled along, spotted the flight of wooden steps and headed down to the beach. But when we stepped on to the sand, there was a surprise in store...

***

"This is great!" Ian said, as he got himself comfortable on the sun lounger. "It's so relaxing and quiet here."

"It certainly is," I agreed.

Stretched out on my own sun lounger in my swimsuit, I closed my eyes and soaked up the golden rays of the warm sun. All I could hear was the sound of the waves gently lapping the shore, the odd cry of a bird and... Ian snoring.

I smoothed on some sun protection cream, then picked up my book.

We were going to enjoy this holiday so much!

***

"Did you find the secret escape beach, Karen?" Dee asked me eagerly, a few days after we'd arrived home.

I was in the garden, pegging out the washing. There's always so much laundry to be done when we get back from holiday, I thought.

"We did," I replied over the fence. "I know you told me about it, but did you and Barrie tell anyone else about this little bit of paradise?"

She beamed.

"Of course we did."

I took a break from my task for a moment.

"How many people was that, roughly?"

Dee looked blank.

"Oh, I don't know. We posted snaps on our social media – we probably have a couple of hundred friends between us. Oh, and we told the regulars down at the pub. And both sets of workmates."

"And they all shared it on social media as well, no doubt," I concluded. "Plus, all the customers in the corner shop heard us talking about it too."

Dee was puzzled.

"What's the problem?"

"The secret escape isn't secret any more," I chuckled. "It was crammed full of people, Dee! There wasn't any space on that beach for me and Ian."

Her face fell. "Oh no!"

I smiled.

"Don't worry. We went to the main beach instead. As everyone had chosen your haven, it was very peaceful for us. So we had our secret escape experience, after all!"

BY: S BEE. PIC: SHUTTERSTOCK CREATIVE

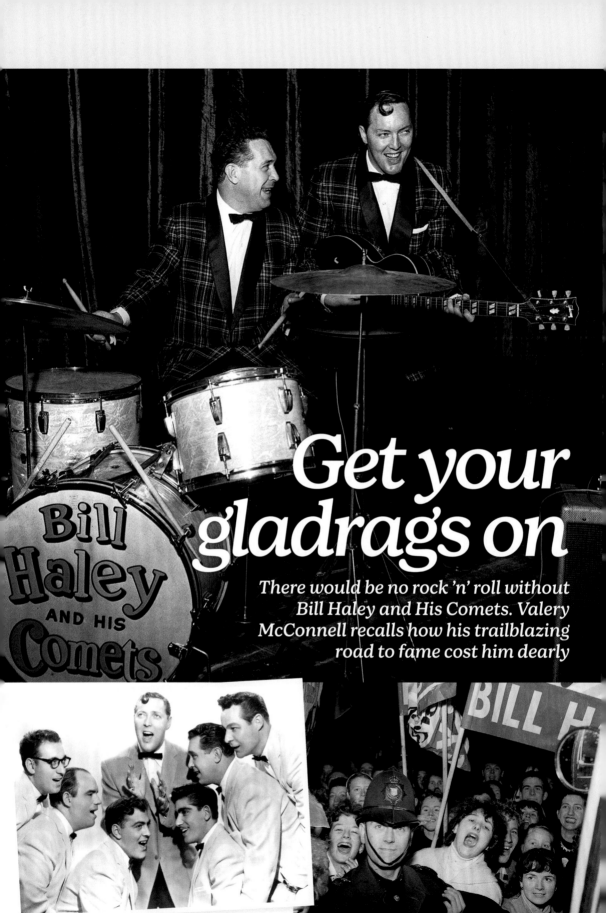

Get your gladrags on

There would be no rock 'n' roll without Bill Haley and His Comets. Valery McConnell recalls how his trailblazing road to fame cost him dearly

Behind the music

Was it time for Bill Haley and the Saddlemen to hang up their cowboy hats? It was 1949 and they had been performing in the same small country venues for ten years. Bill, aged 24 and with a family, DJ-ed on a radio station as a back-up. Unusually for those segregated times, he got to play rhythm and blues – then called race music – and according to his son Bill Haley Jr., "while he was playing his hillbilly music, these R&B songs were in his head. My father decided to integrate these two forms of music".

While Elvis was still a boy, The Saddlemen recorded the R&B song Rocket 88 and became the first white band to cover what would become known as rock 'n' roll. It wasn't a big hit, but when played live the slap-bass beat and sax-driven sound drove their younger audience members wild.

They ditched their stetsons, created a few stage moves and switched from touring country venues to high schools. Bill, picking up on the slang their teen audience used, wrote Crazy Man Crazy, which went into the top 20 of the pop charts in 1953 – another first for a white group playing R&B style.

Teenage anthem
By now called Bill Haley and His Comets, they released Rock Around the Clock in 1954. Then fate stepped in. The producers of Blackboard Jungle, a film about juvenile delinquency in New York, were looking for a track for the opening credits. Its star, Glenn Ford, brought in some of his son's records – and Rock Around the Clock was among them.

It was the first time a rock song had been used in a film, and audiences went wild – jumping out of their seats and dancing in the aisles. Rock Around the Clock became what Frank Zappa called "the teenage National Anthem". It went to No. 1 and

eventually sold 25 million copies worldwide. Bill and the Comets became global superstars.

But while it was the stuff of dreams, there were huge pressures. Bill, married for a second time and with a growing family, was already 31. He'd been painfully shy since a botched operation as a child left him blind in his left eye – hence the kiss curl over his other eye to distract attention. While he smiled on stage, off it, his bandmates remember he was uncomfortable with the adulation and stayed in his hotel room chain-smoking.

And he now found himself having to defend this new 'rock 'n' roll' music accused by parents of causing juvenile delinquency. He commented unhappily, "if that's what I do to these kids, I don't want to do it any more." But he had no choice,

Audiences went wild – jumping out of their seats and dancing in the aisles

swept up in a relentless schedule of recording and touring.

An unlikely idol
Chubby and balding apart from that kiss curl, Bill was not standard teen idol material, but when they toured Britain he was mobbed by thousands of fans at Waterloo Station. As the first American rock star to tour here he had a huge effect on future titans of pop. Pete Townshend of The Who remembers, "The birth

of rock 'n' roll for me was seeing Bill Haley and His Comets – God, that band swung!" It was the same the following year when he toured Europe and Australia.

And yet already Bill's world was crumbling. In 1955 he had met a young singer called Elvis Presley who had told him that when he heard Crazy Man, Crazy he knew he wanted to be a rock 'n' roll singer. A year later Elvis, younger and with sex appeal in abundance, had become the new teen idol.

The hits dried up, and by 1959 Bill's rock 'n' roll star had been eclipsed. His second marriage was in trouble and he was drinking too much. Bad business decisions meant he didn't even have a financial cushion.

He was there first
In the early Sixties he ran away from money problems and his family to Mexico. He married again and was popular in Mexico, while Bill's fans in Europe stayed loyal when he toured. But he felt that America had unfairly forgotten him. When Elvis died in 1977 he told his family, "If you see a headline that the king of rock 'n' roll is dead, don't believe it. I'm still alive."

His drinking became so bad that it all but obliterated his personality. He pulled himself together for a final European tour in 1979 – even playing to the Queen at a Royal Variety Performance. But his wife Martha said that at the end, "It was like sometimes he was drunk even when he wasn't drinking." He died in February 1981, aged just 55.

Despite selling more than 60 million records, Bill Haley can often be overlooked as one of the greats of rock 'n' roll. Yet, he was the one who saw the possibilities of blending R&B, country and pop to create a new genre of music. As Bill Haley Jr. says, "I think my dad would like to be remembered as the guy who was there first."

Being Neighbourly

How would Sheila ever get her lazy husband out of bed?

"**G**ood morning, Sheila," Alf from two doors down said. "Is Ian about at the moment?"

"He's just in the shower," she lied.

Since being made redundant a month ago, Ian rarely got out of bed before lunchtime.

She wasn't about to tell Alf that, though. She didn't want him thinking her husband was a layabout.

I'm sick of making excuses for him

"Oh, right. Only, I was hoping I could borrow his drill," Alf went on.

"Can you shout through the bathroom door? I really want to put up some shelves in the kitchen."

She glanced at the hall clock – it was 7.45am.

Sheila wanted to tell Alf to buy his own flipping drill. He was always borrowing Ian's stuff. But Ian would have a fit if he thought she'd been rude to a neighbour.

Yet if Ian wasn't available, then it was her decision…

With Alf finally taking no for an answer, Sheila wandered into the kitchen to put the kettle on for a cup of tea.

"Got rid of Alf, then?" Tara, her teenage daughter, said with a grin.

"Yes. Why can't your father just get up in the mornings? I'm sick of making excuses for him. I don't know what to keep saying."

Later, she decided to tackle Ian about his extremely long lie-ins.

"You won't find another job lying in bed," she said.

"You should send out your CV – there are lots of other building firms that need tradesmen."

"They don't want blokes my age," he replied.

"They're only interested in youngsters."

He didn't speak again for the rest of the evening. He'd just sat there, staring at the television.

Then, at 9.30pm, he decided on an early night.

The following morning, when the knock came at 8am, Sheila was ready to stop being polite and tell Alf to get lost.

But it wasn't Alf. It was a young man she'd not seen before.

"Hi, I'm sorry to bother you so early. I'm Jake, I've just moved into Ivy Cottage. Do you know it?"

"Yes, I do," Sheila replied, staring into his deep brown eyes.

"The overgrown brambles scratch me whenever I walk by."

"Apologies for that, but they won't be there much longer. I've ordered some tools and they'll arrive tomorrow. But I can't wait to get started on clearing the garden – I don't suppose there's any chance I could borrow a spade?"

"Mum can't lend out tools without Dad's permission," Tara said, appearing from nowhere.

"Ian's in the bath," Sheila said, scrabbling to invent a new excuse. "But I'll go to the shed and see what I can find…"

She returned with a spade, a fork and secateurs. Tara was chatting to Jake and Alf had arrived.

"Is Ian around?"

"No, he's not," Jake replied. Accepting the tools, he winked at Sheila and left.

"Can I borrow an extension cable?" Alf asked.

"My cordless screwdriver has run out of battery. I'm so sick of all this DIY. Do you think Ian would come round and finish my kitchen? I'll pay him, of course, and maybe Jake will need some help with Ivy Cottage…"

"I'll ask Ian when he's out of the bath."

"Bath? He's usually in the shower."

"He fancied a change," Sheila snapped, as she slammed the door.

The cheek of it!

She wanted to tell him to shove his kitchen job but remembered Ian's words about being neighbourly.

Ian wasn't any more impressed with the job offer.

"It's hardly a contract to build a new shopping centre," he moaned.

"Well, you can tell Alf that yourself!" Sheila yelled. "We could really use the money and I'm sick of lying, saying you're in the bathroom when you're still lazing about in bed."

"So tell him something else, then. I don't care," Ian grumbled.

"Why should I?" Sheila snapped.

"See you later!" Tara shouted up the stairs. "I'm off to help Jake with his garden."

"Who's Jake?" Ian asked.

"He's the new occupant of Ivy Cottage," Sheila replied. "He reminds me of you when we first got married – up early, hardworking, and eager to get things done. Oh, and he's young, and drop-dead gorgeous, too…"

He reminds me of you when we first got married

Jake returned the tools the following morning.

"Is Ian still in bed?" he whispered. "Tara told me about him not getting up, and you telling Alf he's in the bathroom. I think I have an idea about how we can get him moving – we need to help each other, and be neighbourly, right?" he winked.

"OK, what's the plan?"

Jake grinned.

"Ian!" he yelled up the stairs. "It's Jake! As Sheila can't get in the bathroom, she's coming round to my place for a shower…"

BY: GILLIAN MCKINLAY. PIC: SHUTTERSTOCK CREATIVE

QUICK CROSSWORD 4

ACROSS
1 Mountaineer's excursion (6)
4 Battle of 1066 (8)
9 Meagre (6)
10 Twice the radius (8)
12 Poacher's quarry (4, 4)
13 - - - few, elite minority (6)
15 Notion (4)
16 Irish poet (5, 5)
19 Learnt (10)
20 Cut – with scissors, perhaps? (4)
23 Short-legged hound (6)
25 Orthodontic device (8)
27 Water boa (8)
28 Sleep-apnoea sufferer? (6)
29 Exact, explicit (8)
30 F in 'TGIF' (6)

DOWN
1 African spear (7)
2 Lacking appeal (9)
3 Northamptonshire village, and 1645 battle (6)
5 In the existing state of affairs (2, 2)
6 Native American axe (8)
7 Paper money (5)
8 Doctor - - -, Marvel film starring Benedict Cumberbatch (7)
11 Cut of beef (7)
14 Was caught in two minds (7)
17 Former name of St Petersburg (9)
18 Demotion (8)
19 Ace (3, 4)
21 Act the part of (7)
22 Ring cycle composer (6)
24 Sceptre (5)
26 Emend (4)

Puzzles

TV QUIZ

1 How many hosts of The Great British Bake-Off have there been?

2 In what year did Coronation Street first air on ITV?

3 Which actor portrayed Inspector Morse?

4 Which TV theme begins with the words: "You know we belong together..."

5 What is the name of René's wife in 'Allo 'Allo?

6 Who played Alf Garnett in Till Death Us Do Part?

7 Name the comedy duo who starred in anarchic hit Bottom.

8 Name Casualty's longest-serving character.

9 Which of these actors has not appeared in The Vicar of Dibley: Emilia Fox, Keeley Hawes, Peter Capaldi?

10 Ant and Dec first worked together on which children's TV drama?

11 Who played Queen Elizabeth II in the first two seasons of The Crown?

12 Who presented TV quiz Blockbusters between 1983 and 1995?

13 Which member of The Beatles narrated the first series of Thomas the Tank Engine on TV?

14 Long-running ITV police drama The Bill was set in which fictional suburb?

15 Which singing competition was the first to feature Simon Cowell as a judge?

Were you right?
Turn to page 182 for the answers

Bedroom Farce

Paula's bedroom makeover was turning into a complete disaster

It had been a lot of hard work, but everything was falling into place.

After years of Rich and I putting up with a dingy, unloved bedroom while we did up the kids' rooms the best we could afford, finally it was our turn.

We had taken a week off work and hired a steamer to remove the old wallpaper, then painted the walls a soothing sage green.

They said there had obviously been a mix-up in the packing department

"We might as well declutter the wardrobe while we're at it," I'd proposed, and two trips to the charity shop later, the doors actually shut properly for the first time in years.

We'd sanded the dowdy old chests of drawers, given them a coat of varnish and added new knobs.

Mum had treated us to bedside lighting to replace the mismatched car-boot-sale desk lamp on my side, and the kids' old Noddy one on Rich's side.

"It's really coming together, Paula," Rich said.

"Yep," I agreed. "Now if you pop over to Textiles Town and collect our new duvet and curtains set, I'll clean the window, run the vacuum cleaner round and put on the sheets."

"And you're sure the duvet and curtains are in stock?"

"I had an email yesterday to say they've put a set aside with our name on it. Oh, Rich, I can hardly wait to put the finishing touches to our all-new room!"

Later, I tore the plastic wrapping off the textiles parcel excitedly. At last, a colour co-ordinated bedroom!

The curtains were lovely, a small leaf pattern in sage green to match the walls. Out came the pillowcases next, more of the sage green leaf pattern.

Now for the duvet cover – with two of us helping, it wouldn't be such an arduous task stuffing it with our quilt.

What's this? I thought, as I opened out the fabric.

"Rich? What on Earth?"

Rich watched as I spread the cover out on our bed.

It was bright pink and adorned with a picture of a cartoon mermaid!

"Blast!" I exclaimed. "They've given us the wrong duvet cover!"

"Don't panic," Rich said. "It's only lunchtime, we can go back and exchange it."

"I can't!" I cried. "I assumed the room would be finished by now, and I've made a hair appointment."

"I thought you cut your own hair?"

"I do, usually. But with the new bedroom and all, I thought I'd make an effort. I've arranged to pack the kids off to Mum's and I was going to cook us steaks."

"You mean we're having a romantic night in?"

Rich hastily started folding up the pink duvet cover.

"Then I'd better get our mermaid back where she came from," he said grinning.

"Would you mind? I'm sorry it means another trip."

"No problem. Go and enjoy the salon."

****

I was feeling great about my new hair. Cutting your own locks was economical, but

It wasn't fair. We'd spent the last of our budget

I never managed to make them swishy and bouncy like this.

"Well, did you get the new cover?" I called, dropping my keys in the dish.

"Not exactly," Rich replied.

"What do you mean, 'not exactly'?"

"Well, they said there had obviously been a mix-up in the packing department."

"Obviously, yes!"

"But then they checked their stock on the computer, and it turns out they no longer have this line. The assistant looked at every outlet, but no-one had any."

"So what can we do?"

"She said, if we returned everything, we could have a full refund."

"But we can't return everything," I reminded him. "I already cut a foot off the bottom of the curtains to make them fit the window."

It wasn't fair. We'd spent the last of our budget on the bedroom textiles, the steaks and my hair.

We simply couldn't run to buying a whole new duvet and curtains arrangement, and we couldn't put back the old ones because they'd gone to the charity shop.

"The only luck we ever have is bad luck," I moaned.

****

Later on, just before closing time, the hair salon boss rang me.

"Those pics you were kind enough to let us take of you, the before and after shots?" she began.

"I emailed them to my boss and he's got back to me. Not to be rude, Mrs Woods, but they're the best advertisement for our stylists that he'd ever seen.

"We'd like to use them in our publicity, if you're willing. We'd pay you £200 plus a complimentary wash and blow-dry."

I couldn't believe it.

"Yes, please!" I gasped. "Just tell me where to sign."

"Rich!" I shouted, as I set my phone down. "Put the steaks back in the fridge. We're going shopping!"

BY: EIRIN THOMPSON. PIC: SHUTTERSTOCK CREATIVE

Do the Freddie!

JD Savage remembers when Merseybeat took the world by storm and Manchester's Freddie & the Dreamers decided to join in the fun

Freddie Garrity, born in 1936, was a football-loving schoolboy. He tried out for Burnley, Manchester City and Manchester United, but his future didn't lie in sport. He left school at 15, taking his first steps into showbusiness five years later. Singing April Showers, he won a local talent contest, his prize an electric shaver (not that he shaved much at the time!). A year later, he started a skiffle group, The Red Sox. Shortly after, he joined The Kingfishers.

The band kept their day jobs, taking time off over the summer to perform at seaside resorts for family audiences. Freddie was a door-to-door brush salesman by day, and one of his clients inspired their next name: "You're just a bunch of dreamers!" He'd changed career to milkman by the time the band took off. When he heard the BBC were auditioning, he said he rounded up the Dreamers and drove the milk float as fast as he could to Television Centre!

The band parodied The Shadows' synchronised leg movements on stage. Their own dancing was much crazier, and little Freddie would leap in the air, his arms and legs flailing. Audiences loved it.

A regular Thursday night slot at Liverpool's famous Cavern Club saw them sharing the bill with The Beatles. Freddie remembered the club's disinfectant smell most of all, remarking that it "must have the cleanest rats".

In 1963, John Barry signed them to EMI Records. Their first single If You Gotta Make a Fool of Somebody reached No.3 in the charts that May. Follow-up I'm Telling You Now climbed to No.2. Yet the band's most requested song at concerts was an album track, Short Shorts.

Behind the music

"Freddie is the only man I know that can sing, dance and remove his trousers at the same time."

A 1964 edition of ITV's Sunday Night at the London Palladium also captured them at their energetic peak. Freddie leaps wildly around the stage, as the band members bounce in the air. After the musicians collapse, Freddie and drummer Bernie Dwyer try their best to prop the guitarists back up. The routine went down a storm, but Freddie realised the visual side of the group was making more impact than the music (he considered their songs to be "crap").

Their visual antics also delighted America, where the band performed on TV in 1965. This led to a US No.1 with the

---

Freddie chased girls in the audience, sticking a feather duster up their skirts

---

million-selling I'm Telling You Now. When a TV host asked Freddie the name of his crazy 'dance', he hastily improvised: "It's called The Freddie." His record company promptly arranged for him to record a single: Do the Freddie, which was also a hit.

But the band couldn't capitalise on their American success. As showbiz-orientated as ever, they had to return to England for a summer season with Tommy Cooper and panto with Des O'Connor.

Little big time
The chart hits dried up after 1965, but Freddie was a natural for children's TV. The ITV series Little Big Time began in 1968, running until 1974. It started as a variety show, recorded in a theatre in front of 500 children. Animal acts

featured heavily, including a boxing kangaroo that took Freddie on.

Series two featured a musical segment: Oliver in the Overworld. Bassist Pete Birrell played Oliver, a grandfather clock who loses his memory. Freddie accompanied him to the Overworld, a strange world of machinery, to seek the Clockwork King's help.

The serial took over 1971's well-remembered third series, also producing a delightful soundtrack album. Overworld characters with their own songs included The Undercog and the fearsome Hungry Drains. Freddie considered this live, weekly musical to be the best thing he ever did.

The Dreamers had split by the time Little Big Time ended, but Freddie reformed them to tour Britain, America and Australia in 1976. He remained a regular panto performer, and became a serious actor – appearing in Shakespeare's The Tempest in 1988. He also performed many more Dreamers concerts, though with none of the original band members.

Freddie died of emphysema in 2006, aged 69. His stage antics made him unique, but many of his songs were better than he gave them credit for. With singles like You Were Made For Me, Over You, Brown & Porters (Meat Exporters) Lorry, and Little Big Time, he left us some real pop gems.

Freddie chased girls in the audience while performing the song, sticking a feather duster up their skirts. When they started chasing him, he realised he'd become a proper pop star!

What a crazy world
The movie What a Crazy World, out that summer, captured their live act for posterity. They perform several songs at a dancehall, including a spirited Short Shorts. Freddie reveals his own stripy boxers and pulls down the other band members' trousers to reveal their shorts. On the EP's sleevenotes, director Michael Carreras wrote that

Minding Her Own...

Mags wasn't really being nosy, was she?

Short story

Mags was apoplectic, and she gave her cuppa a violent stir just to prove it.

"The cheek of her!" she spat at her daughter across the table. "Can you believe she said that to me?"

It was the third time in as many minutes that Donna's mother had relayed the story, and every time was funnier than the last.

Keeping a straight face was by now an Olympic sport, a test of strength and stamina.

"She needn't think she'll be getting a Christmas card from me this year, that's for sure," she said with an angry hiss. "Calling me a curtain-twitcher..."

"She has a point," Donna said with raised eyebrows, doing all she could to hold in the giggles, stuffing her face with a Digestive before a smile had the chance to appear.

"It's not curtain-twitching, it's keeping an eye out."

"Keeping an eye out?" Donna replied incredulously.

"I'm not harming anyone, am I? I just like to know what's going on around me. In this day and age, it's the responsible thing to do. Just last week there was that carjacking in Manchester!"

It's not curtain-twitching, it's keeping an eye out

"That happened 200 miles away, Mum."

"And it could happen on my doorstep tomorrow."

"If you say so," Donna agreed with a sigh.

She'd heard of people becoming eccentric in their old age, but her mother was really taking the biscuit.

It was probably that CSI box set she'd picked up at a car boot sale.

The conversation went round in the same circle a few more times before there was no more tea left in the pot, and only crumbs where a stack of sweet treats had sat before.

"Just try to avoid any more drama," Donna said as she hugged her mother on the doorstep. "I don't have a spare room if the neighbours run you out of town."

"Very funny," Mags replied with an unimpressed purse of the lips as the hug ended.

Mags waved her daughter off until the car disappeared into the distance, before turning on her heels and tutting at the dreadful state of the garden at No.9.

With any luck their rosebush will fall foul of the next cold spell, she thought. Maybe that'd teach the witch inside to keep her thoughts to herself instead of going around making ludicrous accusations about the neighbours.

But with the front door closed behind her and the kettle on for another cuppa, Mags wondered if the fishwife next door actually had a point.

Was she spending far too much time peering out the front window?

It's not like she had anything better to be doing with her time these days.

All her friends were busy doing their own thing, or living on the other side of the country. And there was nothing but repeats on TV these days.

Donna did suggest taking up a hobby to meet some new pals, but that felt like a lot of effort.

Who wants to go to all that fuss and bother of introducing yourself at a book club or knitting group?

Still, she decided to test herself and prove once and for all she wasn't a curtain-twitcher – for the rest of the day, she'd stay as far away from the front window as physically possible.

Life could carry on out there if it wanted to, and she wasn't going to pay one bit of notice.

The kettle whistled and Mags stared towards the net curtains, already tempted to go and have a nosy.

This was going to be a very long evening.

The knock came on the front door after dark and would have startled even the strongest of hearts.

'You didn't happen to see any suspicious activity?' the man in uniform asked

There was no doubt about it, it was definitely the knock of a policeman.

"You didn't happen to see any suspicious activity?" the man in uniform asked after some introductions.

Mags shook her head.

"Not a thing, I'm afraid."

The policeman gave the sigh of someone counting down the days to his retirement.

"Well, if something jogs your memory and you recall something you think may be useful, be sure to give us a call."

"Oh yes, I will."

Mags waited until he was at the bottom of the garden path before allowing the mischievous glint to come out of hiding.

With acting like that, she could give Judi Dench a run for her money.

She'd seen everything the officer was asking about – the two louts who broke into next door's car, the way they sped it down the street and the screaming of the next-door neighbour when she realised just what had happened...

She'd seen it all, and she hadn't said a word.

Nor was she going to.

That'd teach the old bully at No.9. Curtain-twitcher? What a liberty!

BY: SHANE TELFORD. PIC: SHUTTERSTOCK CREATIVE

Puzzle answers

QUICK CROSSWORD 1

Page 150
Across 1. Big Ben, 4. Waitress, 10. Violinist, 11. Acute, 12. Romeo, 13. Twinkling, 14. Gabriel, 16. Eclair, 19. Mullet, 21. Romance, 23. Algerians, 25. Lasso, 27. Naomi, 28. Hugh Grant, 29. Hostelry, 30. Stoker.
Down 1. Beverage, 2. Groom, 3. Editorial, 5. Astaire, 6. Track, 7. Erudition, 8. Sleigh, 9. Pistol, 15. Bourgeois, 17. Lamplight, 18. Reporter, 20. Teacher, 21. Resign, 22. Paunch, 24. Rhine, 26. Shack.

MUSIC QUIZ

Page 151
1. Farrokh Bulsara. 2. Brie Larson. 3 Elvis Costello. 4. David Bowie. 5. Peter Gabriel. 6. Little Richard. 7. Aretha Franklin. 8. Bridge Over Troubled Water. 9. Dionne Warwick. 10. George Michael. 11. Video Killed the Radio Star by The Buggles. 12. Michael Hutchence of INXS. 13. The Bee Gees. 14. Creedence Clearwater Revival. 15. Ringo Starr.

QUICK CROSSWORD 2

Page 158
Across 1. Formal, 4. Offended, 9. Remain, 10. Mandarin, 12. Ring, 13. Rocky, 14. Unit, 17. Single-minded, 20. Going through, 23. Hack, 24. Livid, 25. They, 28. The bends, 29. Solemn, 30. Handsome, 31. Crusoe.
Down 1. Fortress, 2. Ruminant, 3. Avid, 5. Frankenstein, 6. Eddy, 7. Daring, 8. Donate, 11. Norman Wisdom, 15. Bloom, 16. Merry, 18. Ruthless, 19. Cheyenne, 21. Thatch, 22. Screen, 26. Bess, 27. Four.

SPORTS QUIZ

Page 159
1. Fred Perry. 2. Miroslav Klose. 3. Rowing. 4. Basketball. 5. Gary Lineker. 6. Six. 7. 22. 8. Athens in 2004. 9. Diving. 10. Darts. 11. Cassius Clay. 12. South Africa. 13. Fencing and swimming. 14. High jump. 15. Claire Balding.

QUICK CROSSWORD 3

Page 166
Across 1. Fellow, 5. Perhaps, 9. Baritones, 10. Laver,

Can you get top marks in our quizzes?

11. Even, 12. Igloo, 13. Brie, 16. Kittiwake, 18. Inert, 19. Amuse, 21. Submarine, 23. Then, 24. Spare, 26. Pelt, 29. Hitch, 30. Third-rate, 31. Winston, 32. Glenda.
Down 2. Earnest, 3. Late, 4. Wineglass, 5. Pesto, 6. Role, 7. Adverse, 8. Street theatre, 9. Breakfast Show, 14. Linen, 15. Milan, 17. Embarking, 20. Uneaten, 22. Ireland, 25. Putin, 27. Shot, 28. Idle.

FILM QUIZ

Page 167
1. "Rosebud". 2. The Tonight Show Starring Johnny Carson. 3. A horse. 4. Richard Attenborough. 5. Taxi Driver. 6. On the Waterfront. 7. All About Eve. 8. Old Time Rock and Roll by Bob Seger. 9. Ian McKellen. 10. Mary Poppins. 11. La La Land. 12. Rope. 13. Some Like it Hot. 14. Moonraker. 15. The Orca.

QUICK CROSSWORD 4

Page 174
Across 1. Ascent, 4. Hastings, 9. Sparse, 10. Diameter, 12. Game bird, 13. Chosen, 15. Idea, 16. Oscar Wilde, 19. Discovered, 20. Snip, 23. Basset, 25. Retainer, 27. Anaconda, 28. Snorer, 29. Definite, 30. Friday.
Down 1. Assegai, 2. Charmless, 3. Naseby, 5. As is, 6. Tomahawk, 7. Notes, 8. Strange, 11. Brisket, 14. Wavered, 17. Leningrad, 18. Comedown, 19. Dab hand, 21. Portray, 22. Wagner, 24. Staff, 26. Edit.

TV QUIZ

Page 175
1. Six (Mel Giedroyc, Sue Perkins, Sandi Toksvig, Noel Fielding, Matt Lucas and Alison Hammond). 2. 1960. 3. John Thaw. 4. Home & Away. 5. Edith. 6. Warren Mitchell. 7. Rik Mayall and Adrian Edmondson. 8. Charlie Fairhead. 9. Emilia Fox. 10. Byker Grove. 11. Claire Foy. 12. Bob Holness. 13. Ringo Starr. 14. Sun Hill. 15. Pop Idol.